PATCHWORK POETRY
& Other Gibberish

BY THE SATURDAY SONGWRITERS

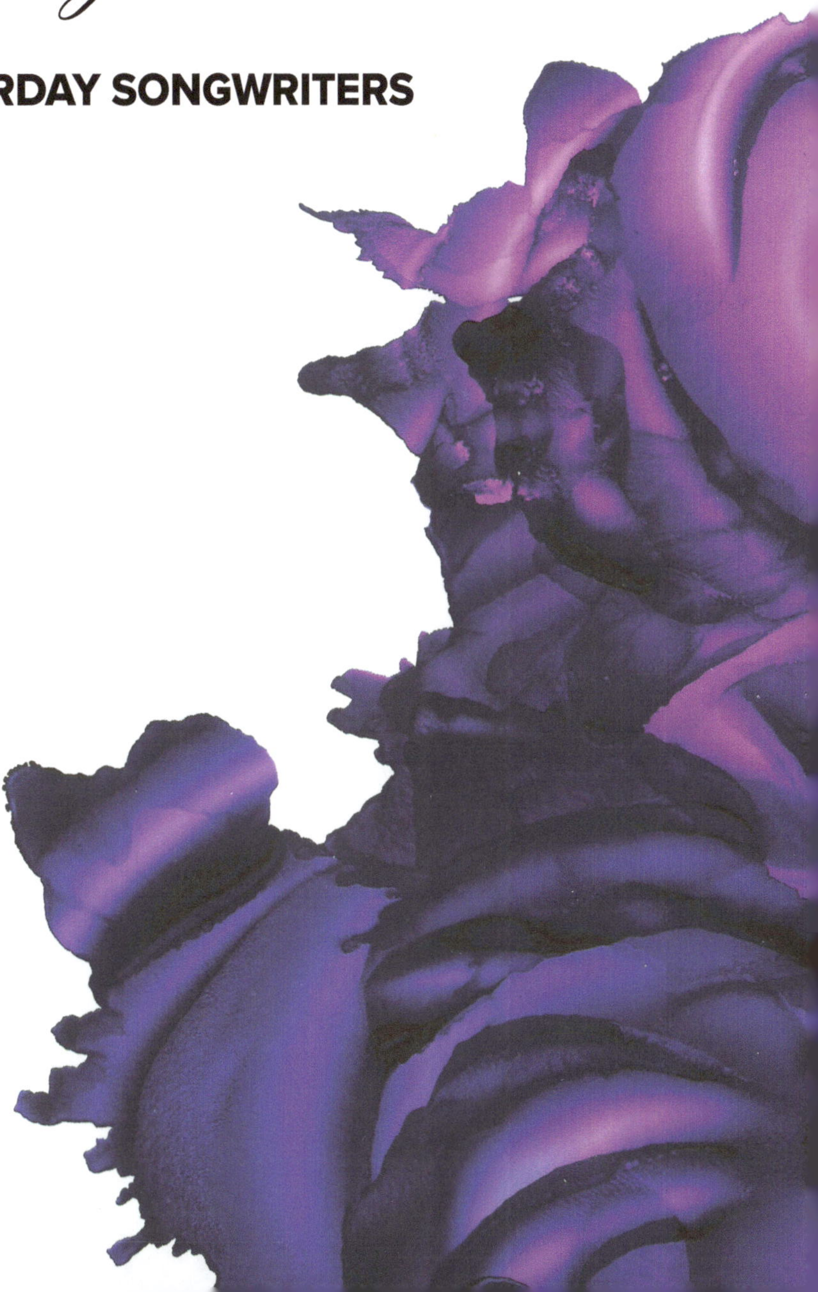

Patchwork Poetry and Other Gibberish by The Saturday Songwriters

Copyright ©2020 by Alethea Kontis and MK Brennan

All rights reserved, including the right to reproduce this book, or portion thereof, in any form.

"green in october" copyright ©2020 by courtney lavender, previously published in *Altadena Literary Review*.

"Poetry of a Pandemic" (p. 23) contains snippets from Snow Patrol's "The Lightning Strike." Original lyrics by Gary Lightbody, ©2008

Edited by Alethea Kontis and MK Brennan

Cover Art: "Sunset Storm" by Denise Denevi
Half Title Art: "Rose Spectacular" by Mel Eatherington
Book Design: Adriana Bergstrom (adriprints.com)
Fonts Used: Source Serif & Proxima Nova

Alethea Kontis
PO Box 512
Mims, FL 32754
USA
www.aletheakontis.com

ISBN: 978-1-942541-33-2

For Gary

The last time that we saw you
was not the last page of the book.

Thank you for everything.

Loads of love,

The Saturday Songwriters

Table of Contents

This Is Not a Eulogy, Alethea Kontis	xii
Blessings from an Isolating Time, MK Brennan	xiv
Saturday Songwrite – Lockdown 2020, Deborah Thackray	1
Ode to Gary Lightbody, Terri Joseph Garrity	2
Voice in the Head, Tihana Šiletić	4
word power, erica dirven	5
home is a song, courtney lavender	6
Chords and Words, Julie Bierlaire	7
Glimpses of the Past, Cindy O.	8
Untitled, Louise Roberts	9
Conduit, Denise Denevi	10
Heart Song, Terri Joseph Garrity	11
As Bright as Venus, Shelley Blair	12
No es Coincidencia / No Coincidence, Corina Oliver	14
Sonnet 2020, Alethea Kontis	15
Meaning, Jana Wiebach	16
Untitled, Camila Alvarez	17
Cosmic Reverie, Faye Kelly	18
Out of Reach, Jana Wiebach	18
Untitled 2, Camila Alvarez	18
A Good and Kind Idea, Julie Bierlaire	19
Ode to Saturday Songwrite, Tihana Šiletić	20
One Saturday Songwriter's Collective Journey, Denise Denevi	21
Transcurso / Course, Corina Oliver	22
Poetry of a Pandemic, Margarita Martinez	23
Orphaned Lyrics, Denise Denevi	24
The Gibberish Heart, Cindy O.	25
No Coincidences, MK Brennan	26
Traveling Companions, Denise Denevi	27
Unidad / Oneness, Corina Oliver	*28*
fireside, courtney lavender	29
Saturday Songs, Darla Dallas	30
Sing to Me, Terri Joseph Garrity	30

Table of Contents

Humanity, Lizzie Ottaway	30
View from the Window, Cindy O.	31
The Hour Before Sunset, Julee Dardeau	32
Untitled, Juliana Flores	33
Some of these Doors, Jack William Finley	34
Colors, Faye Kelly	35
Water and Light, Evelyn Refinius	35
Raindrops in Sunlight, MK Brennan	36
Butterfly Song, Mihaela Berg Divald	37
metamorphosis, erica dirven	38
Spread Your Wings, Jana Wiebach	39
Pleasing View, Juliana Flores	40
Untitled 2, Juliana Flores	41
Untitled, Jane Hopkins	41
Untitled 3, Camila Alvarez	42
Chronic Illness Fighter, Yara Artiles	43
Living the Never, Alethea Kontis	45
Untitled 2, Louise Roberts	46
Captured In Prisms, Alicia Lewis	47
Waves, Juliana Flores	48
Life on Choctawhatchee Bay, Julee Dardeau	49
The Heart of the Ocean, Mihaela Berg Divald	50
Emergence, Mercedes McLaughlin	51
Far Away, Cindy O.	52
Message in a Bottle, Jack William Finley	53
A gentle hope sings me home, Vanessa Power	55
For Truth, Vanessa Power	56
Restart, Tihana Šiletić	57
Container of Truth, Darla Dallas	58
Late Summer Morning, Evelyn Refinius	58
Imperfect Perfection, Yara Artiles	59
green in october, courtney lavender	59
Dog Days of Summer, Vanessa Power	60

SATURN RINGS by Mihaela Berg Divald

Table of Contents

Wait and See, Jack William Finley	62
Eire, MK Brennan	64
November, Jana Wiebach	65
moving to new york, Mel Eatherington	66
A Figure of Speech, yk miyazaki	66
Untitled 4, Camila Alvarez	67
The Pen, yk miyazaki	69
no words needed, erica dirven	69
Insane, Faye Kelly	69
For Haik, Vanessa Power	70
Untitled 3, Louise Roberts	72
The Longest Shadow, Mercedes McLaughlin	72
Sunday Morning Cuddle, Tihana Šiletić	73
Release, Terri Joseph Garrity	73
Fragile Glass, Mihaela Berg Divald	74
Jigsaw, MK Brennan	75
Vessel, Alethea Kontis	77
That Was the Chair, Lizzie Ottaway	78
Satchel of Lockdown Jottings, Lizzie Ottaway	80
Soul Fate, Juliana Flores	82
Underestimated, Carell Casey	83
Waiting, Terri Joseph Garrity	85
Echoes, Alicia Lewis	85
Mom, Jennifer Simone	85
The right words to write about the woman of Nearness (Connection), yk miyazaki	86
mosaic, erica dirven	88
Hiding in Plain Sight, Mary Beth Scholl Maas	89
Permission Granted, Alethea Kontis	90
Masculinity, Yara Artiles	90
Loud Music, Louise Roberts	91
Letting Go, Tihana Šiletić	91
Happy Sadness, Yara Artiles	92
Melody, Margarita Martinez	92

Table of Contents

Love's Screaming, Alicia Lewis	93
My Strength Mihaela, Berg Divald	94
Eons in the Making, Darla Dallas	95
Skipping Act Two, Darla Dallas	96
Desperate and Divine, Alicia Lewis	97
Hearts Beat, Jack William Finley	98
Heart, Spirit, Soul, Mihaela Berg Divald	100
Iuno, Jana Wiebach	101
Untitled, Jack William Finley	102
Back To Earth, Carell Casey	103
Untitled 5, Camila Alvarez	104
Untitled 4, Louise Roberts	104
life, erica dirven	104
I Lost Sight, Sonia Vance	105
For M.O. Thank You, yk miyazaki	106
Saturday 8pm BST, Lizzie Ottaway	107
Curious Collaboration, Vanessa Power	108
A Different World, Darla Dallas	109
lightbody, courtney lavender	110
One More Time Together, MK Brennan	112
The Last Page of the Book, Alethea Kontis	113

SATURN RINGS by Mihaela Berg Divald

List of Art

ROSE SPECTACULAR by Mel Eatherington (half title page) — i
SATURN RINGS by Mihaela Berg Divald — v-ix
CALMING THE CHAOS by Denise Denevi — x-xi
SERENDIPITY IN MAY by Alethea Kontis — xiii
WALKING THROUGH FIRE by Corina Oliver — xiv
SATURDAY SONGWRITE by Carell Casey — xvi
GARY by Anna Lvova — 3
FLAME OF LOVE by Tihana Šiletić — 4
GUITAR ON FIRE by Andrea Worley — 6-7
GREEN EYES OF SWITZERLAND by Denise Denevi — 9
BLACK AND WHITE HEART by Mihaela Berg Divald — 11
FISSURE by Mel Eatherington — 17
CALMING THE CHAOS by Denise Denevi — 22
THE TIRAMISÚ by Anna Lvova — 23
GIBBERISH HEART by Cindy O. — 25
BLUE NEON by Cindy O. — 26
FIRESIDE SESSIONS by Aga Rzymska — 29
WINDOW by Cindy O. — 32-33
LATE SUMMER MORNING by Evelyn Refinius — 40
LIVING THE NEVER by Evelyn Refinius — 44
HANDS 2 by Aga Rzymska — 46
LIFE ON CHOCTAWHATCHEE BAY by Julee Dardeau — 48-49
HEART OF THE OCEAN by Mihaela Berg Divald — 50
SATURDAY SONGS by Lori Throne — 54
THE CURVE OF THE EARTH by Lizzie Ottaway — 63
THE HOUR BEFORE SUNSET by Julee Dardeau — 65

List of Art

MODERN RAINBOW by Mel Eatherington — 67
HANDS by Aga Rzymska — 68
WORD MAGIC AND GIBBERISH by Evelyn Refinius — 76
OPEN HEART by Anna Lvova — 79
EMERGENCE by Mercedes McLaughlin — 84
MOSAIC by Cindy O. — 88
GOLD GREEN by Mihaela Berg Divald — 91
INNER LIGHT by Mel Eatherington — 95
COLOR OF MUSIC by Andrea Worley — 99
REACHING OUT TO YOU by Lizzie Ottaway — 100
REWORKED by Denise Denevi — 107
GLIMPSE by Cindy O. — 108-109
BOOKSHELF by Anna Lvova — 111
ROSE SPECTACULAR by Mel Eatherington — 113
MAN ON MOON by Andrea Worley — 119
GARY by Lori Throne — 139
CALMING THE CHAOS by Denise Denevi — 114-164
SONGWRITERS by Lori Throne — 165
MODERN RAINBOW by Mel Eatherington — 166-167
HEART by Anna Lvova — 170

SATURN RINGS by Mihaela Berg Divald

Contributor Q&A

Aga Rzymska	114
Alethea Kontis	115
Alicia Lewis	118
Andrea Worley	119
Anna Lvova	120
Camila Alvarez	121
Carell Casey	122
Cindy O.	123
Corina Oliver	124
Courtney Lavender	126
Darla Dallas	127
Deborah Thackray	128
Denise Shafer Denevi	129
Erica Dirven	131
Evelyn Refinius	133
Faye Kelly	134
Jack William Finley	135
Jana Wiebach	136
Jane Hopkins	138
Jennifer Simone	140
Juliana Souza Flores	141
Julie Bierlaire	142
Lizzie Ottaway	143
Lori Throne	145
Louise Marie Roberts	146
Margarita Martinez	147
Mary Beth Maas	148
Mel Eatherington	149

Contributor Q&A

Mercedes McLaughlin   150
Mihaela Berg Divald   151
MK Brennan   153
Shelley Blair   154
Sonia Vance   155
Terri Joseph Garrity   156
Tihana Šiletić   158
Vanessa Power   160
Yara Artiles   162
Yoshimi Miyazaki   163

Suggested Charities   166

Alethea Kontis, Editor Bio   168
MK Brennan, Editor Bio   169

CALMING THE CHAOS by Denise Denevi

This is Not a Eulogy

Everyone dealt with Lockdown 2020 in their own way.

Publishing came to a standstill. Conventions were cancelled. Budgets were cut. My cosplay friends made masks. My musician friends played live gigs on social media. My extrovert friends called me on the phone, in tears. My parents battened down the hatches. My little sister stopped talking to me.

As someone who is familiar with the darkness, mine was an altogether different journey. I thrived in solitude. I found meditation. I found spirituality. (I found an allergist!) I reveled in springtime showers, the smell of magnolia blossoms, and the Dharma. In lieu of driving to NASA, I watched the rockets launch from my backyard. I finished one journal and started another. I danced with Adam Ezra every night, wept through Justin Furstenfeld's acoustic sets, and hid in the blanket fort that was Saturday Songwrite.

Those familiar with me and my work know I'm not exactly inconspicuous. I'm the shiny girl who stands out in a crowd, the loudmouth princess who lends her voice to the silent, the forest fairy who leaves a trail of glitter wherever she goes. But in the Songwrite chat I was just another wayward soul tossed upon stormy seas, taking refuge with the man who sings about a Love I Desperately Want to Believe Exists Somewhere.

Snow Patrol has been my favorite band for well over a decade, but I didn't know Gary Lightbody's name before this year. I had no clue how wide and deep and welcoming the Snow Patrol fandom would be. My only wish now is that I had found them sooner.

But I know certain things happen in their own good time. I take pleasure in those little synchronous ironies. The outside world closed down, and my world opened up. The planet suffered, and I healed. One sister walked out the door of my life, and a hundred sisters from every corner of the globe walked right in.

I have watched these women blossom before my eyes, this sangha that used to be strangers. They are smart and sensitive, creative and compassionate. They are brave and wise. They are poets and scientists. They are teachers of children and leaders of men. They travel the world and speak dozens of languages. They create communities within communities, and everything they touch turns to magic. They hold each other up every day, without judgment, without barriers. Every endeavor is a labor of love. *The Fireside Sessions* EP was born out of that love and rose straight to the top of the charts.

SERENDIPITY IN MAY by Alethea Kontis

The Songwriters saved my life this year. I hope this book conveys even a fraction of my gratitude for their continued presence. As difficult as 2020 was for the world, Saturday Songwrite will forever remain a precious memory to those of us who lived it.

In these pages you will find numerous odes to Saturday Songwrite and a multitude of thanks to Gary Lightbody and the band we all hold dear. We have written about lives that were, lives that are, and a Love We Desperately Want to Believe Exists Somewhere.

Perhaps we found it.

May you and your dearest stay safe and in good health.

Alethea Kontis
Space Coast, Florida
USA
October 2020

WALKING THROUGH FIRE by Corina Oliver

Blessings from an Isolating Time

March 21, 2020 was a turning point for me in so many ways. It truly set the trajectory of my COVID-19 induced isolation path in a way that could never have been imagined. Since 2006, I had enjoyed the music of Snow Patrol on and off after hearing "Chasing Cars" on the 2nd season final episode of *Grey's Anatomy*. Admittedly, paying attention to all that was happening with SP's music waned somewhat as life took various twists and turns for both me and the band. That changed in 2019 when I rediscovered them one random day while going through my music catalog. I caught up with what I had missed through videos and new CD purchases, which then led to Facebook and Instagram connections. Most notable among these were Gary Lightbody's announcements of live sessions during the lockdown, including the Saturday Songwrite sessions.

Besides the fun of writing a song every week, the added benefit of the sessions was the community that was created. Individuals who did not know each other before connected through Instagram, Facebook, and email. During the live sessions, we recognized each other's names and started to send messages to our new friends.

A comment on one of Gary's Instagram posts made by Courtney with Xs & ARROWs about using lyric suggestions from SSW (Saturday Songwrite) for her own writing prompted a couple of us to respond saying that we had been doing that. One thing led to another. Friendships were formed, I worked with another songwriter to put together a collection of writings from songwriters as a "thank you" for Gary, a fundraiser in gratitude for those who worked on the EP raised £600 for Help Musicians UK, and others created t-shirts with the proceeds going to charity.

Additionally, a Facebook group was started by Jana in Germany, Erica in Holland, Cindy in Switzerland, and me in the US. It is specifically for Saturday Songwriters as a place to continue sharing their creativity. Original poems, prose, and art have been posted. A #100daysofHeaney project was started that provides an opportunity to appreciate and discuss the works of Seamus Heaney. There is a "Lyric Line of the Week" initiative that provides a phrase for members to use as a prompt for their writing. An "Art Adventure of the Month" has recently been started for those who enjoy painting, drawing, and photography.

This book is a further expression of the community created because of Saturday Songwrite. What started on March 21 led to 11 weeks of songwriting, 12 songs written, and an EP called *The Fireside Sessions* with proceeds going to the Trussell Trust. One more Songwrite session was held in August 2020 so there are now 13 songs and the possibility of an album in the future. While all of that is truly amazing, one of the real blessings of SSW is that the world came together in a very special way during a period of time that was isolating for many. For me, the blessings are immeasurable as I practice my guitar, write poetry most days, and have the courage to work on my own book of writings. While a pandemic has created so many challenges this year, I am grateful that it did provide an opportunity for all that has transpired after one man had an idea of writing a song with whoever showed up on Instagram one day.

May all who read this anthology get a sense of the community that was created and continues to flourish.

MK Brennan
Charlotte, NC
USA
October 2020

SATURDAY SONGWRITE by Carell Casey

Saturday Songwrite – Lockdown 2020

Saturday 8pm BST

Around 2000 people from all over the world

Tuned into Instagram and

United together to suggest random chords & lyrics for a

Remarkable man to make into songs! After the SSWs decided what their favourite tune was (usually number 3), he would

Disappear for an hour and return with

A song using the suggested lyrics and the chosen chords.

You had to be there to believe it—amazing that someone is so talented and could turn them into a song in less than an hour!!!!

Snow Patrol's wonderful Gary Lightbody gave up his time to

Orchestrate the whole event; there was lots of gibberish and

No one knew the end result would be so

Great!!!!

We wrote thirteen amazing songs, five of which were

Recorded and arranged by the brilliant

Iain Archer, with beautiful vocals from Miriam Kaufmann and Graham Hopkins on the drums

Trussell Trust was the nominated charity and received all the monies from our

Epic EP—*The Fireside Sessions*

—Deborah Thackray

Ode to Gary Lightbody

Shine on Gary!
Through song and word and deed.
You nurture our collective souls.
Quick to laugh with a smile so warm it could launch a rocket into deepest space.
Your kind soul radiates love and light which envelops and infuses us through your grace.

—Terri Joseph Garrity

Voice in the Head

Voice in the head,
"You are not creative," it said
Voice in the head
"You are not interesting," it said
Voice in the head
"You cannot write," it said.

A bunch of lies
Swarming in our minds
Not questioned at all
Stopping us
To learn and to try
To love and to reach high
Misleading the faith, hopes and sparks
We are carrying inside
Breaking us down
And leaving us behind
Before we even try.

Instead
Just one grain of courage
Just one word of love
Little bit of kindness
To support a creative light
Is enough to ignite
A seed of warmth and boldness
In a fearful, aching heart.
To give ourselves a credit
With little bit of love
For trying and giving our best
In the moment here and now.

—Tihana Šiletić

FLAME OF LOVE by Tihana Šiletić

word power

my writing
is a cleansing act
an exorcism
every destructive word
spoken
and all aggression
unleashed upon me
is made undone
by the beauty
love and light
radiating
from the pages
of my notebook
with my fountain pen
i am taking back
my life
one word
at a time

—erica dirven

home is a song

home is a song
that tingles from scalp to sky
that sings a synapse stampede
breathes a thick-lunged lightning

home is a storm of song
that flashes down in flood
relieves a parched, stagnant silence
breaks humidity's fever

home is a siren song
horizon ever-shifting

—courtney lavender

GUITAR ON FIRE by Andrea Worley

Chords and Words

Harmonies are universals,
We know it,
We proved it, so many times,

We all have different stories,
Some of us play other instruments,
Some of us got their voices,

But harmonies are there,
In our ears,
And in our heart,
« Perfect chord »,
« Do majeur »
« Chord of C »,
Or simply beauty,
Chords can have so many names,
But harmonies are in our ears,
And in our heart,
We can all hear it,
We can all feel it,

On our Thursdays,
On our Saturdays,
We can all hear it,
We can all feel it,

Harmonies and words are our country,
our same sky.

—Julie Bierlaire

Glimpses of the Past

Glimpses of the past
in shapes of memories
flooding through this clear mist
that pinches my mind with needles

Glimpses of the past
telling of times
when laughter was true joy
and heartbeats jumped not limped

Glimpses of the past
almost forgotten
but never really vanished fully
hiding in the pages of ancient books

These glimpses of the past
are part of me
have shaped my life and who I am
maybe they appeared for a reason?

—Cindy O.

In that spring day
I fell in love

With the forest
With the flowers
With the wind

With the sunset
With the stars
With the moon

And with you

—Louise Roberts

GREEN EYES OF SWITZERLAND by Denise Denevi

Conduit

A Conduit of Connection
A Bright and Shining Star
Like A Light Unto A Moth
Attracting Us From Afar

We Made Lyrical Lemonade
From Sour Covid Lemons
Planting Seeds of Hope
We Wrapped Them Up in Love

A Gift to Those In Need
A Gift to Us Indeed

A Conduit of Connection
A Bright and Shining Star
Like A Light Unto A Moth
Attracting Us From Afar

We Formed Sacred Bonds
Friendships of the Heart
Deep and True Connections
Feelings Weak and Strong

We Found our Voices
Putting Pen to Paper
Ink to Art
Pick to Strings
Lyrics to Verse

We Found the Light in the Darkness
We Waited for the Dawn
We Felt the Curve of the Earth
We Will Live ~ Unforgotten

—Denise Denevi

Heart Song

Speak to me in ancient tongues
When nothing became everything
Penetrate my darkened silence
You are the earth beneath my feet
Hold me tightly in your arms dear
You are seared into my soul
Finding solace in our memory
Gentle hands and sun kissed lips
Your song forever in my heart
My heart forever in your song

—Terri Joseph Garrity

BLACK AND WHITE HEART by Mihaela Berg Divald

As Bright as Venus

by Shelley Blair

Twilight had come in and the first stars were beginning to appear as Grace crossed the road to the bus shelter, dragging her suitcase behind her. She carried a guitar case in her other hand and had a handbag with a long strap slung across her body. The walk from her home had been a short one, but it felt like it had taken forever. Finally, she reached the stop and sat down on the bench seat, feeling slightly weary due to the weight of the luggage she had been carrying. She looked into her handbag to make sure everything she needed was there. Passport—check. Flight confirmation email and boarding pass—check. Mobile phone—check. Purse and credit cards—check. Her trusty MP3 player—check. Yes, she was all set. She looked at her watch: ten minutes to go.

Earlier that evening, she had met her four best friends at their favourite restaurant for dinner, which had turned out to be a fairly emotional occasion as it would be the last time they would all be together for some time to come. There had been hugs, kisses, tears and promises of emails, phone calls and occasional visits. Now, though, she was alone at the bus stop. She wore a silver chain around her neck with a glass star pendant threaded onto it. The lights from the roof of the shelter made both the star and her long, flame-red hair look like they were glowing.

"How lucky am I to have friends who care enough about me to see me off like that?" she thought, rolling the pendant between her thumb and index finger as nerves started to kick in. "Am I crazy to leave them? Why am I doing this?" Then she remembered why: she was following her dream.

———

Right from childhood, Grace had always been the artistic one in her family. Growing up, she was rarely seen without a camera, sketch pad or guitar in her hands. Much of her creativity was inspired by her other great passion: road racing, which she had grown up around. She and her parents attended as many races as they could during the season and their main family holiday each year was to the Isle of Man for the TT, where they stayed with her aunt Jo. Every year, Grace filled entire films and, as she grew older, memory cards with photos from each event the family attended (the TT was, however, her confirmed favourite) and when she was fourteen, she decided that this was what she wanted to do for a living. Over the years, she took as many photography courses as she could and eventually landed a job with her local newspaper as their sports photographer.

After four years there, the opportunity she had been waiting for came up. One evening, Jo called her with the news that a job was available at the Island's largest newspaper. It only took a brief conversation with the rest of her family to convince Grace that applying was the right thing to do, so the following day, she did just that and a fortnight later, she flew over to the Island to an interview. Three weeks after that, she received a phone call offering her the position, which she immediately accepted. She was on her way to fulfilling her stated ambition of becoming "the female Stephen Davison"—a reference to the top road-racing photographer she wished to emulate.

―――

The arrival of the bus brought Grace out of her dream. She checked her watch again; the ten minutes had gone by in what seemed like the blink of an eye. She took a look around her and then quickly gazed up at the sky. More stars had appeared and she spotted Venus almost directly above her. She picked up her luggage and boarded the bus, showing the driver her ticket as she walked down towards the back. Picking a window seat, she set her cases at her feet and her handbag on her lap and settled in. She took one last look at her hometown and smiled to herself. It was about to become part of her past, but she was okay with that, because she knew that the future she was heading into was a bright one. "As bright as Venus," she thought. With that, she lifted her MP3 player out of her handbag, put her earphones in, cued up one of her favourite albums—Snow Patrol's A Hundred Million Suns—and rolled off into the night to meet that future.

No es Coincidencia

Antes de la oscuridad,
la oscuridad
Sin horizonte
Qué haría
Navegué en la incertidumbre
pero el tiempo fue mío.

Ahí estuve
No por casualidad
Lugar correcto
Momento preciso
Como un faro
Con su rayo de luz para aliviarnos.

Sentimientos encontrados
Para buscarme
Para intentar encontrarme
No lo entendí en ese momento
Gracias
Estaba volviendo
a ese lugar donde quiero estar.

No Coincidence

Before the dark
Darkness
No horizon
What would I do
I sailed in uncertainty
But the time was mine

There I was
Not by chance
Right place
Right time
Like a beacon
With its ray of light to relieve us.

Mixed feelings
To look for myself
To try to find me
I didn't understand it at the time
Thank you
I was coming back
to that place where I want to be.

—Corina Oliver

Sonnet 2020

I could write sonnets all about a smile
Sing out my lonely truth into the night
Shout loud I love yous from across the miles
Spark every match until two hearts ignite
But who would love me in this poisoned world
To stars my wishes fly like hopes with wings
In all this noise I am but one strange girl
Who hides herself among much stranger things
The world outside is drowning in despair
A million screams like neverending rain
No solace to be found, no safety there
And echoes in the dark won't ease the pain
      What saves my soul from getting lost anew?
      The light that shines in me
            It could be you

—Alethea Kontis

Meaning

Random words and phrases
Dancing in the air
Racing through glass fibres
Fast as lightning in the dark sky.

Words like
Life, love, light
Thoughts echoing
In a thousand minds.

Phrases like
Hold on, hold close
Feels swinging
In a thousand hearts.

Random words and phrases
Spinning round and round
Alone they mean nothing in and of itself
Together they mean the world for us.

—Jana Wiebach

My mind is
Wide and wild
Always escaping
To places
Where the chaos
And confusion
Are just an echo
Among the stars.

—Camila Alvarez

FISSURE by Mel Eatherington

Cosmic Reverie

mercury gets warm
venus lights up
earth seas dance
mars creates dust storms
jupiter moons align
saturn twists its rings
uranus swirls the clouds
neptune winds increase
even pluto gets close
only to admire
your flaming
and majestic light

—Faye Kelly

The planets converge
And the stars collapse
To make our celestial bodies align.

Two moon dreamers
And a glittering love
Through space and time.

—Camila Alvarez

Out of Reach

I see you
Standing in the rain
Water pouring down your face.
I'm wondering
Why don't you
Come to the shelter
Right here.

I see you
Standing in the blinding sun,
Your shape trembling
In the shimmering heat
Longing
For cover in the shadow
Right here.

I see you
Shivering in the cold night,
Alone in the darkness
Under the broad starry sky.
Waiting.
Why won't you
Come closer?

—Jana Wiebach

A Good and Kind Idea

When I was a kid,
I was scared.
Were you scared?
Like me?
Alone and scared, in front of the blackboard,
Alone and scared, in front of a blank page,

I was scared all the time,
At school,
At home,
I was scared to be me, I have few keys now,
But sometimes I am still trying to figure it out,

But music,
And words were already there, for me,

Today, music and words are still there,
At home and in lockdown,
You had this idea,
To put together our music, our words
And slowly a community is created,
And it works,
Because we were not scared and we were together,
Free to be ourselves,
We could write,
We could laugh,
We could share,

And it simply works,
Do you know this ancient thought?
Aristotle, apparently, used to say,
We are smarter together,
Well, we can say, we are happier together,
Creative and kind

It was your idea,
A simple, a beautiful idea,
You are the musician,
You put the songs together,
Fast and with magic,
But it made sense to us,

We were not scared anymore,
We were not alone anymore,
We could create and be ourselves,

I don't know much but I can tell you,

It's rare,
It's precious,

It was a good and a kind idea,
I am going to end here,
With a simple and warm
Thank you,
To you, to all of you

—Julie Bierlaire

Ode to Saturday Songwrite

Red paint and colors of fire
Announce the dearest online date
Saturday is here to inspire
And lifts our spirits to create.

Crackling noise of the well trained fire
On the bookshelf looking smart
The gang is somewhere there to lift us higher
And give our best to help you start.

Yellow notebook on the desk board
With four versions of suggested chords
Each melody you record
Is fighting for our hearts to be adored.

Connecting chords together to astonish
Line on forehead comes and goes
And here comes little bit of gibberish
Your funny way to compose.

Fiery voting
For a few minutes
To choose 1, 2, 3 or 4
Gives us melody to work on.

Lyrics passing through the screen
Sad or happy, yet full of hope
You write down the ones you have seen
Our hearts are bouncing, connecting us all.

Four pages filled, spelled right or wrong?
It doesn't matter, but your face says it all.
You burst to laugh to an awkward comment
And even use it in a song.

Funny giggles makes us happy
Your weird faces even more
Getting close to the screen
To catch a lyric, big or small.

Break has come
You have to go
Will we get two songs in an hour?
Or is that too much to ask for?

The clock is ticking
Excitement is at its peak
Words you are using
Each week are unique.

There's a mess in the head
You said
Creative mess
If I might add.

High notes makes you wonder
But you still use them in a song
Chorus like a thunder
To make a song even more strong.

Another musical gem from the heart
So beautifully woven together
From people far apart
Giving their best altogether.

—Tihana Šiletić

One Saturday Songwriter's Collective Journey

Sheltering In
Collectively
The Entire Planet
From this Covid-19 Pandemic

Each of Us ~ Individual Stories Waiting to be Told
Each of Us ~ Individual Voices Wanting to be Heard
Collective Embers Taking Hold
Parts of Self Long Forgotten

And the People Waited ~ And the People Stayed Home
Disconnected, Afraid, Lonely, Grateful, Angry, Confused
Fearless, Isolated, Energized
A Collective Consciousness of Chaos

And Then One Day
A Body of Light Appeared
Among the Chaos an Invitation
Come Light the Flames of Peace and Love and Music

Was it Serendipity? Happenstance? Law of Attraction?
Matters Not ~ Because We Came
From Germany and from France
From Switzerland and Japan
From England, Russia and Croatia
And me from the good old USA

Every Saturday
We Came
We Created
We Laughed
We Cried
We Shared Moments in Time and Across Time and Through Space
Remember Bob and Doug?

And We Called Ourselves Snow Patrol and The Saturday Songwriters

—Denise Denevi

Transcurso	Course

Y busqué mi voz
Y canté otra vez
Y esperé con ansias
Y olvidé todo
por un instante
Y en la melodía
mi ser viajó
Diversión irradiada
Mirada bondadosa
Cálida voz
Y una sonrisa olvidada volvió a dibujarse
Y una lágrima
nubló mis ojos
Alegría, gratitud.
Y un grito interior clamando por salir
No se atreve
Pero lo hará

And I looked for my voice
And I sang again
And I waited eagerly
And I forgot everything
for an instant
And in the melody
my existence went on a journey
Radiated fun
Kind look
Warm voice
And a forgotten smile drawn again
And a tear
clouded my eyes
Joy, gratitude.
And an inner scream crying out
Dare not
But it Will

—Corina Oliver

CALMING THE CHAOS by Denise Denevi

Poetry of a Pandemic

March 11 – Virus detected in NM
The planet's last dance.

March 13 – National emergency declared
Just overwhelm me.

March 17 – First daily song
Connect the dots.

March 19 – First acoustic gig
The only noise.

March 20 – "Hi everybody. How's it goin'? I thought we could write a song together? See how it goes. Maybe make it a regular thing. No pressure ... Seven o'clock, Saturday, tomorrow. Join me."
The safest place found.

March 21 – First Saturday songwrite— Dance With Me.
Something was bound to go right.

March 23 – Lockdown begins in NM
Broken pieces.

March 27 – Sick
Just overwhelm me.

Sept 30 – Still sick
Just overwhelm me.

THE TIRAMISÚ by Anna Lvova

Moonwalking toucans. Flying stars. Sideways panda-monium.
BB-8 (where'd he go, anyway?)
Industrial Light & Magic and an ever-slacking George. Squeaky chairs.

A fire that burned nothing when everything else was in ashes and instead gave life.
Rocket launches. Q&As. Clapping for the NHS.

Backwards numbers. Hearts of three.
The perils of technology. The wonders of technology.

Laughter. Tears. Song.
A community born, an EP made.

Does he have any idea of the life raft those Saturdays became?
When the sun refused to rise, they were my

Daybreak.

—Margarita Martinez

Orphaned Lyrics

I wrote a magnificent poem today
One of many magnificent poems I've written
While driving in my car
Miles upon miles
Inside my head

Now I'm home
And my magnificent poem
Has somehow vanished
Into an unknown space
Inside my head

Like all those song lyrics
Never seen
Never heard
Abandoned and orphaned
Floating somewhere in space

Where detours and dreams collide
Distant moments melting like ice
Taking flight for sure this time
Let's call it night but don't go home

Random lyrics strung together in harmony
I'll remember these days forever
Just like an old friend
Darkness came knocking on my door again
Is it paradox or parsimony?

Found the sun while you were shooting for the stars
Breaking through the darkness
Shattering these illusions of despair
Quantum moments collide like iridescent wavelengths

Remember me Now
Remember me Then
Remember me When
Forget me Not

—Denise Denevi

The Gibberish Heart

The sound of metal strings on wood
Serenading through the silence
A broken heart that is still whole
Embracing me inside of it.
A different world has unveiled its face
A world once known but then suppressed
A world of sounds and words that touch
My soul in motions yet unknown.
A sea of images soft and far
Of people, places, things I miss
Appear, enriched with new ones
Yet to be understood.
The melodies of broken pieces
Fill in the gaps of solitude
A symbol for my changing times
The broken heart stands for all of that.
One word without a meaning
Creates meaning in and of itself
Three syllables of clever beauty
Changing worlds and calming minds.
It unhooks many unthought thoughts
And picks them up to show to me
A different side of who I am
Explored but given up eventually.
Some collapsed dreams and hopes
Reshaping now to something new
I find myself finding myself
Losing myself in the spell of you.
Some struggles now forgotten
Joys and feelings unfold again
These letters without a meaning
Mean more to me than words can tell.
The broken heart that hugs the word
I'll place on top of mine, my friend,
The sound of metal strings on wood
Will now be a companion again.

—Cindy O.

No Coincidences

There are no coincidences
I have often thought
Wasn't totally sure of it
Not a concept easily bought

Then this year proved it true
With too many circumstances
Leading to a new endeavor
Really, what were the chances

A long time separation
From a once familiar sound
Came abruptly to an end
When the world was shut down

New ways of connecting
To share creative forces
Brought together songs of hope
Through collective voices

The leader of the group
One of clever wit and wisdom
Happened to stroll past my view
And in the wake, I'm left numb

There are no coincidences
I now know that for sure
What were the chances paths would cross
During each one's day adventure

—MK Brennan

BLUE NEON by Cindy O.

Traveling Companions

You—The Doctor
Your Guitar—The TARDIS
We—Your Companions

Week After Week
A New Journey
Where Would We Go

Destination Known
Yet Unknown
Battling The Algorithms

Who Will Be Seen
Who Will Be Heard
Pick Me Please; It's My Turn

Week After Week
Anticipation Growing
Let's Board This Ship

Got My Ticket
Got My Lyrics
Even Got A Brand New Pen

It's Gary O'Clock
Waiting, Watching
For The Red Live Screen

There It Is
Now It's Time
First It's Chords
Next Is Lines
Please Pick Mine
Just One Line

Really That One
Strange And Odd
Oh That's A Great One

But So Is Mine
Try Again
Ten More Times
He's On Page Four
Time's Almost Up
Damn It's Over
Like She Said
Not A Damn Word
Well Maybe Next Time

But Next Time Didn't Come
Well At Least Not Right Away
The World Turned Darker

Empty Streets No More
The People Protested
The Buildings Burned

We Came Together
Orphaned Songwriters
Supporting One Another

Waiting For Your Return
Hoping You Would Return
And Then You Did

Announcements Came
Our Music Release
One Last Saturday Songwrite

It Was Joy And Sorrow
All In One
And Forever All For One

We Are Orphans No More
We Are Finding Our Way
We Are Finding Each Other

We Miss Our Songwrite Days
We Miss You Dearly
The Chair, The Gibberish

The Moments We Shared
That Meant The World To Us
And Changed Us Forever My Dear

—Denise Denevi

Unidad

Hilo invisible
acortando las distancias
Almas conectadas

Un experimento
Pausa. Vacío.
¿Lo habría imaginado?

Lugar seguro
para atreverse
Nadie juzga, todos animan.

Corazones bondadosos
Sentimientos compartidos
La música nuestro idioma

Orgullo. Gratitud.
Aquí estoy
repleta de alegría

Oneness

Invisible thread
joining the distances
Connected souls

An experiment
Pause. Empty.
Would we have imagined it?

Safe place
to dare
Nobody judges, everyone encourages.

Kind hearts
Shared feelings
Music our language

Pride. Gratitude.
I'm here
full of joy

—Corina Oliver

fireside

the fire crept in close
jumping roads and ridgelines
crawling through the canyons

i packed everything you ever gave me
clothes, CDs, books
badges, pendants, whistles

each object a symbol
of expression,
our mutual obsession

it's the best i could do
to keep you

—courtney lavender

FIRESIDE SESSIONS by Aga Rzymska

Sing to Me

Spirits lifted by infinite grace
So high there was nothing but light
Only the brightest colors
Starlight in the day
Sunshine in the night
Magic in your voice

—Terri Joseph Garrity

Saturday Songs

Serving as a safe place to fall
All smiles from coast to coast
Trusting in the process
Unguarded love of music
Ready the lyrics wanting to be heard
Dream of dreams today & tomorrow
As we connect becoming more
You unfiltered

Sipped on silliness
On the shelf is our fireplace
Nothing but lazy days
Going to Mars & back
Sweet & bittersweet goodbyes

—Darla Dallas

Humanity

You may never know your own true grace
As you placed your arms around our darkness
You may never feel the face-to-face
Isolating on distant shores
You may never see the rainbow arcs
Nor breathe the amber sweetness
Listen
You may never hear the joy which falls
And savour that
You may never know your own true grace
As you placed your arms around our darkness
You may never know your own true grace
That saved my fettered life

—Lizzie Ottaway

View from the Window

Looking out the oversized window of my childhood living room
The rugged mountains present themselves
Majestic, old and still
As if purposely and perfectly chiseled by some unknown hand
They stand there, always have, always will, a constant.
Smooth snowcaps flowing
Just as a stream of consciousness
Down the ancient glacial paths
Dug out by this other force of nature.
A fluffy cloud, just one
Envelops the tip of a peak like a pillow
Breaking up the jagged lines of the creases.
Then the sunset dips everything in color
First pinks then oranges and reds
Turning the whites and greys into fire
A world before me aflame with light.

—Cindy O.

The Hour Before Sunset

When the rain stopped,
the sun, gulls, and pelicans all returned for a sunset show.
They brought their friend Rainbow,
and the clouds were tickled pink that they were all together again,
and the waves applauded their beauty, in the hour before sunset.

—Julee Dardeau

Gentle arms are wrapped around me
and emerge me from the dark place
I'm already used to
allowing the light to get in
to awake the colors
I thought no longer exist

—Juliana Flores

WINDOW by Cindy O.

Some of these Doors

Some of these doors will always be open
Some of these doors don't lead where you thought they would
Some of these doors should never be opened
Some of these doors hide secrets you're not meant to know
Some of these doors are more than you bargained for
Some of these doors are not the way out
Some of these doors hold riches beyond your wishes
Some of these doors leave scars that will never heal
Some of these doors are rainbows of endless hope
Some of these doors are more than you'd ever want
All of these doors look just the same

—Jack William Finley

Colors

We lay on the green grass
Among the yellow wild flowers
Under the orange and purple sky.

You look at me with your blue eyes
And when your pink lips touch mine
My cheeks get so red.

My hands go from your black hair
To your soft and white skin
Under your grey shirt.

And all that I can feel
Are the beats of your golden heart
And the colors of our love
A beautiful work of art.

—Faye Kelly

Water and Light

Water falls
In a thousand drops
Running down the walls
Hope the rain won't stop
Gentle and cool
Touches to the skin
Filling nature's pool
And our hearts again
If sun will shine
Through the water prism
The light will perform
A colourful session

—Evelyn Refinius

Raindrops in Sunlight

The salt air smells sweet
With thoughts of times gone by
The rhythm of the sea draws me back
Colored memories with rounded edges
Riding the waves of mixed emotions
Wellsprings of love in the dusk of night

The rhythm of the wind dances with the trees
Fills the empty frames of yesterday's dreams
Images flashing through the years
Of my way to you before you go
The stormy heat, thunder in my heart
Flashes of lightning calling in the darkened sky

Dancing in the sunshine of your smile
Glimmers of hope in the fading hours of day
Your return igniting my soul
The ashes of the fire stirred
A small spark bringing light to the night
Intentions this time to be brave

Walking along the sandy shore at dawn
Raindrops in sunlight lift the sadness
Gentle tears, shimmers of dreams
For the love this time around
Forged in tender heartache, simple joys
Your arms an unexpected blessing

—MK Brennan

Butterfly Song

Is this Mask of beauty you are wearing,
covering all the pain inside?
When I say I am, in a shallow way, I'm fine,
How can I define, my pain is truly mine?
Is it just the things we don't want to see?
Does it matter just look on the outside,
not the real me?
Perfect look, smile within the pain,
cracking from the inside, torn, crushed body,
hard to play this game.
If they don't see it,
they say it doesn't count,
broken pieces of my heart,
They still cause the pain when I hear their crushing sound.
While I struggle to survive one day more, I don't need your pity, your approval,
I know I'll get through it all.
Every morning Sun I'll greet with grace, believing my angels are here and guide me through all of this.
No need for small talk, if you don't understand,
I'm not lonesome in my small world,
got everything I need, my precious love, my one and only, my whole universe.
Just be kind from a distance and let us be.
Let our fragile wings fly high,
as long as the universe decides,
it is time to say goodbye.

For Lupus Warriors
—Mihaela Berg Divald

metamorphosis

chrysalis

the lone years
needed for healing
felt like
wasted ones to me
now i understand
that just like winter
as a time of rest
and quiet renewal
prepares cherry blossoms
to show their abundance
to the world
my isolation
was time spent
in a chrysalis
getting ready
to emerge
and spread my wings

i can hover

these wings of mine
are carefully crafted
out of stainless steel
and glass
infinitely delicate
yet infinitely strong
their weight
poses a challenge
but i can hover now
and will learn
to fly
eventually

—erica dirven

Spread Your Wings

Hello my little ladybug
Red as blood and black as ebony
Come rest on my wrist
Before you fly away.

Hello my little butterfly
Distracting with wing's shining colours
Hum a melody for me
Before you fly away.

Hello my little dragonfly
Dancing in the summer's heat
Whisper a secret to me
Before you fly away.

Hello my little hummingbird
Flapping your wings so blazingly fast
Sing me a song
Before you fly away.

—Jana Wiebach

LATE SUMMER MORNING by Evelyn Refinius

Pleasing View

If you could
see yourself
the way
I see you
you would know
how hard it is
to control
the overwhelming
urge to kiss
your sweet
and lovely lips

—Juliana Flores

My dreams
are like wings
that help me
to escape
to you
every night
and for
a single moment
the distance
disappear
for me
to get lost
in you

—Juliana Flores

A distant memory of tender moments,
In an alternate reality of another world,
So close, yet so far, trudging
to get to the other side
Not knowing what awaits us
Taking the leap, having faith
in something we hardly know,
trusting only our instincts,
Time flies by if only we
could hold on to this for
longer, so we can get
lost in this time that we
cherish, feels like another dimension
The path may be long but every
Step taken is a step closer
Where all will eventually fall
into place

—Jane Hopkins

Alone
I don't pretend,
I don't lie.

Alone I am,
who I am,
I do what I want.

I can laugh,
I can cry.

I can dance,
sing, scream.

Alone
I can fly.

But with you,
I can be and do
all that,
and also touch the sky.

—Camila Alvarez

Chronic Illness Fighter

You're not weak for crying
Or having lost it all.
You got sick and
Got taken advantage of.
None of it
Was your fault.
Everyone left
When you could barely move,
When your health abandoned you
And your finances got screwed.
You found friendship in strangers
While "real friends" stabbed you in the back,
You found out that love must be proven
With damn good acts.
It took a long time to heal
Enough to get back to life,
To start working and move
Away from everything
That harmed.
You still cry but jeez
You're strong as hell
For doing that.
You silenced the pain
And started from scratch,
pills and positive thoughts
Could dress up the darkness
So you could see
The light.
With gratitude and optimism,
Even while carrying traumas
You go through life.
Your deep understanding and boundaries
The strongest points you
Could ever have.
Cry when you have to
As tears clean up your soul.
Your light
Will never be again
Turned off.

—Yara Artiles

LIVING THE NEVER by Evelyn Refinius

Living the Never

So how would this happen
It's not like before
You can't just show up here
And knock on my door
No candles are lit, love
The sun is still high
And my dreams of you, love
Aren't done passing by
Just hang on a minute
While I get this straight
You promised me time once
I know that you'll wait
The next time we speak, love
The walls will be gone
You'll hear every word that
I say from now on
I'm safe here in dreams, love
They don't hurt at all
They won't disappoint you
They won't let me fall
In dreams I live free, love
To be my own muse
To dance in the rain, laugh
as loud as I choose
I'll revel in moonbeams
Chase storms till I'm old
And you'll never stop me
From loving the cold

I'll sing when I want to
And not when I must
I'll hide in this house full
Of rainbows and dust
As long as you stay, love
In dreams safe and sound
I can't make you hate me
For being around
We'll never be angry
Or argue or fight
We'll just lie in bed here
And talk through the night
And each word imagined
From me and from you
Won't have to be real, love
For it to be true
Our story's a dream, love
Like shadows in May
That fade with the dawn's light
Forgotten by day

—Alethea Kontis

HANDS 2 by Aga Rzymska

Thunder rumbles
Waves break
Stars fall
The moon rises
Gardens bloom
Clouds form
All that
When your hand
Touches mine

—Louise Roberts

Captured In Prisms

There's a desert in my eyes
There's an ocean in yours
Mine expands the gold glint of
time through your fingers
Yours is the cool dip of ocean waves
that refreshes my soul
The ebb and flow of sand and tide
Underneath your quiet shyness
Beats an intensely feeling heart
She plunges into darkness
Turning it to color splashes
Captured in prisms
You dance in circles around her
Waves crashing into words
Interspersed with explosive crackles of delight
Joining them together
Sand and tide

—Alicia Lewis

Waves

You are the deep
and angry ocean
that eats me like
a hungry animal
and drown me
into your blue

And after seven
seconds of panic
and madness
I let myself
be filled with
your beauty
and vastness

—Juliana Flores

LIFE ON CHOCTAWHATCHEE BAY by Julee Dardeau

Life on Choctawhatchee Bay

The colors are so vivid before sunrise.
The clouds are hung like art, in nature's Sistine chapel.
My favorite times, predawn, sunset, and the darkest of night,
like when you are far offshore in the deepest water,
when you clearly see all the stars of spirits gone before us, and meteors dart, stars fly.
In the bay you hear mullet jump and plop,
and dolphin release a puff of air to exhale,
and occasional tail slap for their mates to signal it's time to come along, or herd bait.
Shrimp boats murmur with patience as their Rocking David nets
appear like angel wings in the deck lights, glowing across the water.
In the moonglow a Blue Heron squawks for undivided attention.
Thank you for all these years Choctawhatchee Bay,
I will return to you when God calls me home.

—Julee Dardeau

The Heart of the Ocean

On the bottom of the deep blue sea
As dark as shadows around me
His beauty is a curse no one wants
Doesn't matter how beautiful he was
He is shining through the waves
Glowing in the dark, doesn't matter is it a day or night
Full of secrets
Hidden so deep
His beauty no one can keep
He is precious, lovely as can be
Long time ago he was someone else's history
Proudly took his place around young woman's neck
Deceive her with his eternal love
But it was just a glow
Surface of colours, dark purple, blue
Did she know how much he was untrue,
His beauty never fades
Even laying in a deep blue ocean
He can't hide away...

—Mihaela Berg Divald

Emergence

The sea brims with tears
of weeping angels swept by mistral winds
Their terrible perfect cries pierce the air
Like a prayer
Hovering over rough waves and floes
Halcyon seas herald the solstice
Stormy shadows set sail on wings
Revealing the finale of fears
Silver-tipped curls of towering waves
crest and quake
Thunder-clapped shocks of sound
gifting effervescent energy
in a percussive wake
Beneath a canopy of scintillating stars
in reverential awe and with full breath
exhales the fire-born fowl
sparking sleepy fires
Golden-flame coils rise to nip angelic toes
Echoes of melancholy escape
Mirth fills their empty space
Ash rains like half notes sung
in a penetrating grey song
Winds serenade the long arc of the smiling
shore

—Mercedes McLaughlin

Far Away

You sit in your shattered glasshouse
Viewing your life in these shards
The pieces can't be put together
Your tears let down your guards
And I can't hold your hand through this
I can't make it untrue
I can't fly across the ocean
But, you know, I'm still here for you.

The darkness inside you is crippling
The chaos rises to your head
These flames find no hope or reason
Only panic and sadness instead
And I can't hug your soul or your body
I can't lead you through
I can't fly across the ocean
But, you know, I'm still here for you

Your happiness grows into the future
A white promise forever held dear
A new life is born in this distance
Your smile just seems so near
And I can't kiss your cheeks of roses
I can't give the stars to you
I can't fly across the ocean
But, you know, I still love and miss you too.

—Cindy O.

Message in a Bottle

I toss my heart and precious thought into a cyber sea
Message in a bottle, for anyone to see
I thought it was directed to whom it was to be
But now, I see, how lost it was to everyone but me
Fickle strands of fiber optics, pulsing impulses
Connections disconnected
Missing direction, karmic insurrection
Illusion of global connection
Tragic disaffection
Impulsive application
Mathematic dislocation
Speed of light
speed of sound
speed of thought
round and round
hearts and minds reaching out
through endless seas of noisy white
chaotic confusion
whipping too many sails
though too many empty spaces
Full of longing faces.

—Jack William Finley

A gentle hope sings me home

I.

When breathing was hard
I would sing to catch my breath

Lost on that ocean of grief
Alone on my own tiny raft
of memories and brokenness

The rise and fall
Soothing as a mother's embrace

You are loved
You are loved
You are loved

II.

Sending up a flare
Holding on to what's already gone
Emotions still white-hot on my tongue
The dry mouth of a bad dream
Grief like a blanket on my shoulders
Paper hearts folded in my hand
This landscape unfamiliar

Inside I am still raining

III.

Coming home is harder now
Remembering our last careless day
All the things we left unsaid
My spring-loaded heart catches in my throat
Holding the moon in the palm of my hand

This will always remain

These pages once were wood

IV.

Feel your way back
This is where we begin
A roadmap through these thoughts
Somewhere there is still an ocean
Waves that tug at my feet and all that I am
Our story now a myth
Just these few words, a raft, your voice
My heart like a fist

A gentle hope sings me home

—Vanessa Power

For Truth

I am devouring poetry
because my soul is starving for truth
And I am too weak
to wade through an ocean
Of words
Searching

These small drops on my tongue
The sidewalk now a darker shade
This reflection in a puddle
enough to remember

That words have power

And power is a splintering force

Hope is never a shadow

Curiosity is a softer place to start than anger

A coin has two sides, flat
Or spinning on its edge becomes
A round orbiting sphere
This same door
the way in or
the way out

And I am squinting.
Beyond my fear.
Trying to focus past this pain.

I am wandering
lost in the desert
Searching for Rumi's field

Praying for those first drops of rain
on my tongue

—Vanessa Power

Restart

Treetops are bathing in the sun,
over parked silent cars,
dancing birds are having fun,
no worries on their minds.

Do you recall a summertime
Bare feet in the sand
holding hands, no sense of time
now pushed apart unplanned.

Safety of the shore
Like an invisible embrace
Gives me a simple comfort
In trying to remember your slowly fading face.

Empty coastal walk
mantled in the glittering stars,
I miss our funny talk
and your fingers softly playing a guitar.

Vastness of the ocean
Breaking us apart
Will I understand my mixed emotions
And feel again a warmth of your heart?

Time has come to hear the silence
And feel the stillness of the night
Only working with love in alliance
To this world we can bring more light.
And bring the Earth to restart.

—Tihana Šiletić

Container of Truth

A fire needs a container a safe place for it to stay
The passion reflects its blue green light upon the broken glass and shimmers
ever so slightly, aiming at the truth
Devouring tiny breadcrumbs, devouring them to keep her feet on the ground!
Swallowing them whole
Aware of the wisdoms not earned
Every view has a vice
Tripping over the truth can be
Terrifying
The fall happens quickly
The fire burns for all time
The fire and the shade trip upon a beautiful genuine
Place
To Stay

—Darla Dallas

Late Summer Morning

Can I capture the silence of this morning
A moment so peaceful and calm
This feeling of new beginnings
And finally letting the past go
A moment of freedom
When everything still seems possible
so hold in and keep it close to the heart

—Evelyn Refinius

Imperfect Perfection

    Baby, look me in the eye. Why are so you scared of showing me who you truly are inside? I don't need you to shine all the time. Perfection doesn't exist, baby. Don't fall into that trap. Baby, show me the demons that still live in your head, the things that broke your heart. Let me dance with your shadows, so my own can kiss your scars. Baby, life is not white or black. We've both done wrong and have hurt in life. I know you see me as a beacon, as a stunning guiding light... But baby, I'm truly flawed and also am as dark as the night. You're not perfect but neither am I. Why don't we accept each other, ourselves, as we are? I don't want to change you and I wish you'd see yourself through my eyes. You are a mixture of iron and glass. And I could never love you the way I do if you weren't just like that. Let's breathe and pray under the sun. Acceptance and self-love are key and, sooner rather than later, you'll find out.

—Yara Artiles

green in october

the desert wind heaves into the valley
like clockwork
sidewalks ticking
with the tumble of crackling leaves

in LA we call fall
fire season
we mark seasons by scent
by slant of the sun

in morning you might find a leaf
limp, alone
90 degrees
and green in october

—courtney lavender

Dog Days of Summer

I.
These feet have followed this path more times than I can remember.
I'm thinking about heads of pins
angels pirouetting on pointe
Eyes of needles
with those patient camels
Squeezing like some infinite spirit into flesh
(We'll need that needle for repairs later)
Each stitch bringing us closer to death
The unraveling
The rip in the fabric
Frayed seam
That gauzy veil
Curtain, like a wall
Metaphors, like tiny parts of an intricate clock, moving the whole universe.

II.
It rained again today.
And the crickets are louder having had their winged instruments washed clean.

III.
It is the dog days of summer
We lay on the damp grass
side by side
A little bit buzzed
A little bit stoned
Listening more than talking
Translating the stories of the night sky.
The Morse code messages of fireflies

If you were a question
It would be open ended
Never a simple yes
(Though that is the answer I catch glancing sideways)
Never a simple no
(Though my tattered heart fingers the key)

IV.
Those dogs know a sunset that we've not yet seen.
High-pitched and curious
The scent of mystery
It's in their DNA to track wonder.

V.
And with all of this
It comes down to
This hand on
This chest
The gentle rise and fall of sleep
The skittering shut eyes of dream
This slow rhythm
This is the mark of time and thresholds crossed.

These feet on the path
My world spinning
Coming home
Needle in hand.

—Vanessa Power

Wait and See

Fall is near
Jack Frost nipping at its heels
Winter is fast approaching
The land of ice and snow
Days grow short and dim
Visions narrow cold and grim
The amber light and warmth of crackling fires
thoughts turn to melancholy things
But the tree of life is vast and timeless
From the fish at the bottom of the sea
to the birds soaring high above the mountains
It's roots cover the Earth
It's branches touch the sky
The spark of life pierces the night
And leads us through the darkness
Spring is just around the corner
Waiting quiet and patient in the shadow of sun drenched summer days
Just beyond the horizon
Winter eyes drift and dream
Be Strong. Be Calm. Wait.
The dawn of light and life are not so far away
The Sun will come again
The world will bloom
Just wait
And see

—Jack William Finley

THE CURVE OF THE EARTH by Lizzie Ottaway

Eire

The distant land called her home
To a place she had not been
It was, however, in her blood
In ways not truly known
Her soul was stirred
With the first glimpse of the green
The ancient stones spoke of a past
Where her ancestors once toiled
The soil, the air, the water
All held her in their arms
Loving touches of welcome
Greeting a long-lost daughter
Come sit by the fire
Make yourself at home
No need to go anywhere
It is time to just be
Breathe in the history
Embrace the wisdom shared
Know that you are one with us
Druids, Celts, ancestors all
Our story is yours to keep
Feel it in your heart and bones
Heritage cannot be denied
It is the fiber of the soul

—MK Brennan

THE HOUR BEFORE SUNSET by Julee Dardeau

November

Digging deep, going back
Where is the curve?
Where is the turn?
Where is the point?

Always
It has always already been there
Like the hedgehog awaiting the rabbit
Like the keeper awaiting the visitor
Like an uneasy answer lingering in the air
Before the question was even asked.

You have always already been you.

—Jana Wiebach

moving to new york

i gorge my long-starved heart
on landscapes, on lushness
naked and made shameless with the privation
of dust and flatland,
scorpions and scorching sky and a thousand shades of beige
it devours hills and forests, frogsong
and autumns and field after field
of late-tasseled corn or thick-packed snows,
ice-laden branches, hushings of winter
and mad riotous springs.

drunk on Adirondack lakes and summer,
drowsy with memories and sunsets
warmed like gold on water,
it returns plumply to my chest
and sighs the sigh of one contented.

—Mel Eatherington

A Figure of Speech

Outside my window
The universe announces early spring
On the trail of a devastating loss
A shadow of tomorrow's mourning
My head needs wrapping, coddling even
Trailing behind
My trailblazer heart
Already sees me claiming Calton Hill

— yk miyazaki

Doesn't matter
How dark
Some days
Can be
Only the sound
Of your voice
Create a rainbow
Inside of me.

—Camila Alvarez

MODERN RAINBOW by Mel Eatherington

HANDS by Aga Rzymska

The Pen

I want to be the pen
in your perfect mouth
you hum the precise chord

I want to hear the bliss
of soaring music
illuminating joy

I want to be the pen
you bite again as
you ponder melodies

I remember that bite
gentle on my breasts
your dreamy caresses

you hold my memory
your mouth favors me
with a practiced kiss

I am that perfect pen
in your perfect mouth
I am contented

—yk miyazaki

Insane

In this world
Full of madness
And craziness
I'm someone
Who is only insane
For your
Exquisite eyes.

—Faye Kelly

no words needed

come into my embrace
and baptise me
with your tears
chest to chest
your body tells me
how you feel
my heavy heart
mirrors yours
and breathing as one
our bodies sync
to find peace
within

—erica dirven

For Haik

I.
The absurdity of it all
Is the one-sided text message

Arguing with myself
Trying to get an answer that wouldn't come.

We'd had a movie date.
At The Guild, our usual.

"So, no movie then?"
Was the beginning of my monologue.

II.
I've often played with the idea of "here" and then "gone"
Mainly when thinking about inanimate objects
Those things that become a reference point for directions
Letting someone know they are going from neighborhood, to street, to house.

There is a big tree on the corner, turn left
You'll see a blue gate; I'm the next house on the right
That red barn in the field—we're about half a mile further down the dirt road

Then one day
They cut down the tree
They paint the gate green
The barn is burned to the ground

And our directions change to
…remember that big tree?
…remember, there used to be a barn?
…remember?

A person is different
A person is here and there and here (heart)

You don't meet a person and turn left or right
Though the direction of your life may be changed

And like neighborhood to house, acquaintance becomes friend
A reference interwoven in stories

Remember that movie we saw?
Remember that time at the park?
Remember that amazing meal?

Remember?

Remember.

III.
And so, you are here (heart)

You are an éclair with a good cup of strong coffee
You are Pad Thai
You are all-you-can-eat Indian food buffet

You are a movie at The Guild
A conversation about NPR, PBS, or Nova
That quirky little question about the English language,
 "why this word—here?"

You are classical music
You are Nina Simone
You are a silly text message in the middle of the night

You are stale cigarette smell on clothes
You are a quick profile sketched during a meeting

You are a walk in the park

You are a dog in the car

IV.
How many times
Had we stood each other up?
Later saying, "I love you anyways—check in tomorrow"

How many times
did one of us get stuck at work or was one of us too tired after work?
 "I love you anyways—check in tomorrow"

How many times
did the couch hug one of us too intimately
so that leaving the house was no longer an option?
"I love you anyways—check in tomorrow"

How many times…?

"I love you anyways—check in tomorrow"

How many times
have I wished over the last three months that I'd gotten a text about tomorrow?

How many times
have I wished I could exchange one of our other missed dates for that Monday night?

I'd give you a dozen of those postponed tomorrows to replace that monologue of texts that ends with…
"If you are alive, please text me. Everyone is worried about you."

And still, I love you anyways…

—Vanessa Power

The Longest Shadow

Be my first light in the last dark
Share this warm bed and open book.
Bare your heart, shed a tear
Grieve with me, the gods will hear.
Weaving tales with flax and thread
Passing under and over the words we read.
Closing our eyes as the longest shadow shortens
My moon and stars shone 'til morning.

—Mercedes McLaughlin

Magnetic
Lovely
Stunning
Gorgeous

Dreamy
Stellar
Adorable
Sublime

Are just
Ordinary words
To describe
Your perfect eyes

—Louise Roberts

Sunday Morning Cuddle

Sunday morning cuddle
Just a distant memory,
In my head a stormy muddle,
Is taking away my energy.

Still feeling warm neck kisses,
In your long embrace,
Is breaking my heart in pieces,
With you being out of this place.

Your arms kept me safe,
In the hug holding hope,
I held onto that,
As it was the only tightrope.

Crackling sound on an old radio,
Is playing your favourite song,
Miles apart, dancing on the tiptoes,
I never thought it would make me so strong.

—Tihana Šiletić

Release

Dig deep
Down to the very root
The deepest breath
The mightiest exhale
Another tiny piece breaks free
Exposed to all and made for none
You write as if no one is watching you

—Terri Joseph Garrity

Fragile Glass

Glass,
On the edge of the table, thin and fragile
One inch you move it, it will go down,
It will crush into tiny pieces
(pieces that can never be found)
Pieces
You can never get back together
Even if you try
Something will be missing
Something like truth or lie
I had all plans in my mind
Nothing came as I thought it would
I don't plan any more
I don't dare, only if I would
Learn to live, nothing will be as you wish for
Or maybe it is?
You just wished for something more.
I am that glass, standing on the edge
Fragile, terrified to be broken down
Because I know I will never be found…

—Mihaela Berg Divald

Jigsaw

Pulling threads through the passage of time
Weaving the fabrics
Gossamer webs
Plates of armor

Fumbling around in the dark for the light switch
Following a path
Clearly laid out through the years

Looking back at puzzle pieces
Turn them over one by one
Where are all the edges

Holding on and letting go
Truth in being
Truth to self

Filling in the blanks, taking chances
Wandering unknown streets
Bright lights and shadowy alleys

Becoming real can take a lifetime
Or so the sages say
Ever changing yet ever new

Flowing along with the ebbing tide
Pieces of flotsam
Riding along, floating away

Holding on and letting go
Truth in being
Truth to self

Holding grace for what has been
Pain and joy
Mirror reflecting all

—MK Brennan

WORD MAGIC AND GIBBERISH by Evelyn Refinius

Vessel

Every wish I've made to now
Has been for you and only you
You'd pull me up aboard your ship
And sail me off to somewhere new
Every man in every book
Has been this wish in some small way
Every dream I've had each night
Has brought me hope for each new day
But after years of looking to
Horizons from which no one came
Of listening into the dark
And hearing no one call my name
I do still dream, for dreaming is
The thing that keeps us all awake
And reaching for those stars, that moon
Affects each choice I strive to make
So here I stand, a vessel full
Of wishes that will never be
I've chosen one bright star tonight
The wish I wish will be for me.

—Alethea Kontis

That Was the Chair

Dandelion clocks
Butterfly kisses
Pheasant warns, cuckoo calling
A place to be
'Though my head is full of doubts
I sent you a postcard from here
Sunset glows, purple skies
And finding my peace in the woods

Broken-hearted, shattered pieces
I never wanted this to end
I've lost you now
But candles have memories
Facing up to the afterlife
Plant a flag, take the rest of the day off
Although life is wasted on me
It'll all be waiting for you

Under your spell
I can fold my pain away
Hold my hand across the ocean
And I will see you in the real world
Don't be so capricious
Old ways of being
I've only seen you cry that once
Are you happy?

One day I'll ask you to decide
If I'm fragile or simply frail?
Looking for healing
Amongst the oyster shells
Diving down, drowning
Veil over my eyes
Fire snuffed out, scant swifts still fly
As the robin sings again

—Lizzie Ottaway

Satchel of Lockdown Jottings

Tall tales
Rekindle woe and torment
Eavesdrop on my senses
Pull the shutters in
Unbridled attachments
Magical objects
Open hands mean grace and mercy
Ten things in my pocket

Am I being selfish?
Not wanting this to end
The longest summer nearly over
Creating problems that don't exist
In those fleeting moments
This did mean the world
Should just be enough
As we move in parallel lines

Swamped by bitterness
I have few words for you
Talking to a screen for six months now
Seeing myself from above
Unheard and sorrowful, I'm out of syllables
You even took my favourite vinyl
Breathe in, don't be duped by all of this
Step into my own truth

The season moves on
And firelight reveals my path
Hazy mornings beachside
Looking out for curlew feathers
Your tousled hair snags
Momentary shafts of sunlight
Exhale, I listen to music to feel safe
Don't miss the quiet ones

I know it's backwards to me
It's still real to you
Call out the last thing on your mind
Palpable ebb and flow
Piles of Post-it Notes on my table
Give me the fear a little bit
It all seems like 'Mrs. Dalloway' here
Where are we now?

I feel edgy tonight
Brim-full of sadness
Am I failing at life?
I should shower my head
It's like you're in the room with me
Good enough for sparkling water
Bereft of connectivity
Last ditch, one more time

You can do this
Don't go, please stay
This is not the finale
'Though I'll remember every moment
Our collective story
Spreads the kindness
Everything that's on your mind
Tell me how you feel

Shouting and raging
I've done my best
Keep showing up and mind yourself
Go for it
This was unimaginable
Join in, stay, stand together
Let's not lose the intensity
My own cool gang

Behave and stay focused
Disarranged, sense the pinch
How do you sleep?
Still safe at home
I'm already in mourning
Why are we even still talking here?
Trying to see the beauty in all things
Is this normal?

'Cos I could love the bones of you
Missing your spider fingers
What was I thinking?
Take a punt
Those pale, expressive eyes
Reflect our essence
I, too, believe in humanity
Can you hear me now?

Still scrabbling for the light switch in the dark
Grant me a muted mind and a peaceful heart
Playing snakes and ladders, always losing
Self-sabotage
Disarmed and unravelled
Heard your name in the haar
Listen in tones and colours
And I will think of you

Oh, don't do that
Be a cheerleader for each other
I'm taking a detour
Which reminds me
This is probably way too high
It won't work, it's ridiculous
Voiceless mouthing a silent movie
What's that?

Lean in, I want to tell you a secret
Can I whisper it?
How was I to know we needed you
This joyful playfulness
It's endearing
Let's start with the gibberish to get to the good stuff
I could dote on you
Done it again, haven't I?

Can you see my fault lines?
My scars are filled with clay, not gold
Extinguish the fire, open the door, release me
As I punch my hands through the darkness
I will pine for you, knitting rainbows
But there can be no sparkle jar
That's as glorious inside
Don't tell me to go after all of this

Thinking what might be lost gets you through
Our season of Saturdays
And our stories have heart
Months of second chances
Elated now
A single strand of candescent hair
Shimmers in scattered radiant light
As I write my morning pages

Dappled patterns
The sun has warmth
Yet casts a longer shadow across the earth
Times of rageful protest, blazes, grief
Halo of piebald gossamer threads
Birds grow quieter, pressed flowers in my book
In the air above the cool, mossy woods
I spy a kestrel

The whiff of Autumn can make me sad
You have a joyous lit-up smile
In pockets of calm and sweetness
You spoke to me so clear for hours
A laugh that made me laugh
I hear you, fall asleep, voice in my head
But I might be beyond repair
This is exhausting

What if this goes upside down and inside out?
Be who I am, not who I want to be
Truly soothing
Invited into your world
Grey, silver, titanium
There's a lot to be afraid of still
Together we can learn the value of many things
Each other's person now

—Lizzie Ottaway

Soul Fate

There's someone
somewhere
lost in this world
who is broken too

Trying to put
her pieces together
and find the path
towards you

The stars will guide her
through oceans and time
and you will know it's her
when your destinies collide

She will be the one
that will heal
your bones, your soul
and light your heart

Will protect you
from everything
end your pain with kisses
and calm your mind

Take you through
fields and forests
fit you in her arms
never let you alone

Then finally you will know
how it's like to be loved
how it's like to be full
how it's like to be
at home

—Juliana Flores

Underestimated

they tried to make us hate ourselves
tried to make us hate each other

they underestimated us
underestimated the power of love
the power of love

like magnets
pulling ever closer
upsetting all obstacles
every challenge
each imbalance
inexorable

they underestimated us
underestimated the power of love

they tried to pile on distractions
divert attentions
but they underestimated us
underestimated the power of love

simple kindnesses, tender touch
sweet silent actions impacting us
stronger than bombs
put all your weapons down
bury them deep in the ground
let them sleep harmless
because this is sheer madness
a tantrum

they tried to make us hate ourselves
tried to make us hate each other

but they underestimated us
underestimated the power of love
the power of love
the power of love

—Carell Casey

EMERGENCE by Mercedes McLaughlin

Waiting

Surrounded by stillness
Enveloped in solitude
She sits under the evergreens
Waiting for the noise
The roar of an open heart
Just one beat
Followed by another
Everything is possible now

—Terri Joseph Garrity

Echoes

Love holds me
Like knotted branches
In the small hours
Drenched in love
By ways and means
Hand in glove
With untold secrets
The roots of you
Like distant poetry
Breathless
Spinning out
Restless hearts
Without a doubt
We're just a jar of memories
Echoes of your touch

—Alicia Lewis

Mom

Time came to a screeching halt
My pounding heart and shallow breath is all that's heard
I scream for help as if anyone could hear me
Holding your life in my hands though unsure what to do
Moments felt like years waiting for them to help you
"Move aside" they said
Crawling back in horror, I watched your life slip away
Praying I'd see your soul float up to heaven
Forever hoping I had blinked and missed

—Jennifer Simone

The right words to write about the woman of Nearness (Connection)

My job has always been to protect you.

When you were only four years old, I allowed what I thought was an act of kindness. I wanted to make your life easier. I wanted to help you grow from that extraordinary little girl you were back then into the extraordinary woman you are today.

My act of kindness failed. My action caused you pain throughout your life, and for that I am truly sorry. That was not my intention. My intention has always been your happiness.

When you were four years old, you went to live in a place that was not very safe, around people who were not very kind, who did not know what to do with differences. In their world, everyone looked the same, had the same skin color, and had ordinary names.

Your names were different, your skin color was different, your eyes were slanted, and your hair was thick and coarse. There was nothing they could do to change these things. The only thing they could change for you to be more ordinary was your name. They gave you names they could pronounce, that sounded just like theirs.

Your beautiful-just-right-birth-name was replaced with another one. You never claimed that name. You always looked over your shoulder, wondering who are they calling?

―――

I have been giving this a great deal of thought. Besides your name being taken away, something else happened to you because you were only four years old.

Even though Mommy was a grown up and knew this was happening for the "best," still she felt shame, unworthy, and bad.

No one in your family was bad—not Mommy, not your little brother, not your daddy, and most of all not you. You, as the little four-year-old girl, saw how bad Mommy felt, and like a good girl you claimed her bad feelings instead of the name they gave you.

If there was a bad that happened, it was that Mommy's shame became your shame.

Do you remember who you were before this happened? Do you remember that fierce two year old little girl when Mommy wanted you to take a nap? You were not tired, you argued with her, and you bellowed, "NO!"

You have always been so strongly capable of standing up for yourself.

Your name was changed to "protect" you. You were innocent. You were loved. When you took on Mommy's feelings as your own, heaven cried.

(To right this, I whispered a promise to you.)

You would one day reclaim your name.

As a grown up, in a court of law, that's what you did. You took back your name. No one will ever take this name from you ever again.

You truly are a woman of Nearness, of connection.

—yk miyazaki

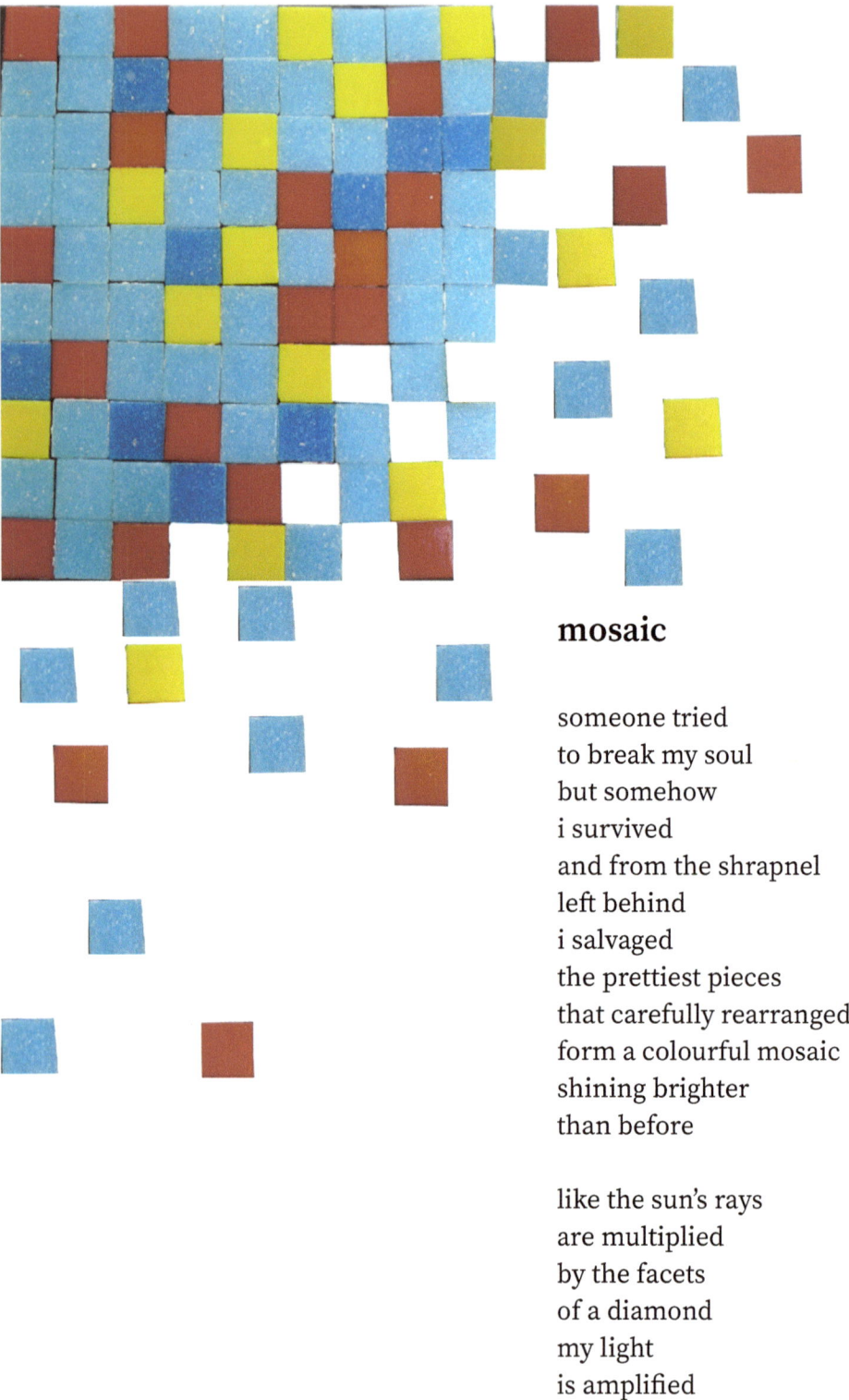

mosaic

someone tried
to break my soul
but somehow
i survived
and from the shrapnel
left behind
i salvaged
the prettiest pieces
that carefully rearranged
form a colourful mosaic
shining brighter
than before

like the sun's rays
are multiplied
by the facets
of a diamond
my light
is amplified

—erica dirven

MOSAIC by Cindy O.

Hiding in Plain Sight

We have been hiding in plain sight
All these years
You and me
We can't stay away
We've tried
But then a chance meeting
Sets us in our orbit again

We've had days of grace and days of pain
All these years
You and me
Holding hands when no one is looking
A flash of love when our eyes meet
Long weeks without you
Days when you couldn't call

And yet the completeness of us never wavers
All these years
You and me
The softness in your eyes still there
The feel of your warm skin on mine
The kiss when we have to say good-bye
I never want to be without you

—Mary Beth Scholl Maas

Permission Granted

It's okay to watch the fireworks
You didn't buy
To eat the strawberry
You didn't plant
To love the rain
You didn't pray for
To warm yourself by the fire
You didn't build
To sing along to music
You didn't compose
To accept the love
You didn't dream of
It's okay
To live this life
You didn't choose

—Alethea Kontis

Masculinity

We kept telling men
How to be strong.
"Don't cry in front of others,
Don't you dare to feel love.
You were made to fight and hustle
Not to make love."
Some of them
Unfortunately believed
Those words.
They bang hoes and have no loyalty
Except for money and bros.
Deep inside, though
They feel alone.
Their spiritual side
Perfectly hidden
Needs to feel a safe drug.
Real love.
The one that can cure it all
And accelerates your growth,
The one that helps you regenerate
When things really get fucked up.
They need to open their eyes
And realize society's
Always been flawed.
Only that way they'll see the truth
Is rarely ever told.
They want us to be apart
In war.
But our nature's inherently social
And we'll find a way to heal
This shattered Earth.

—Yara Artiles

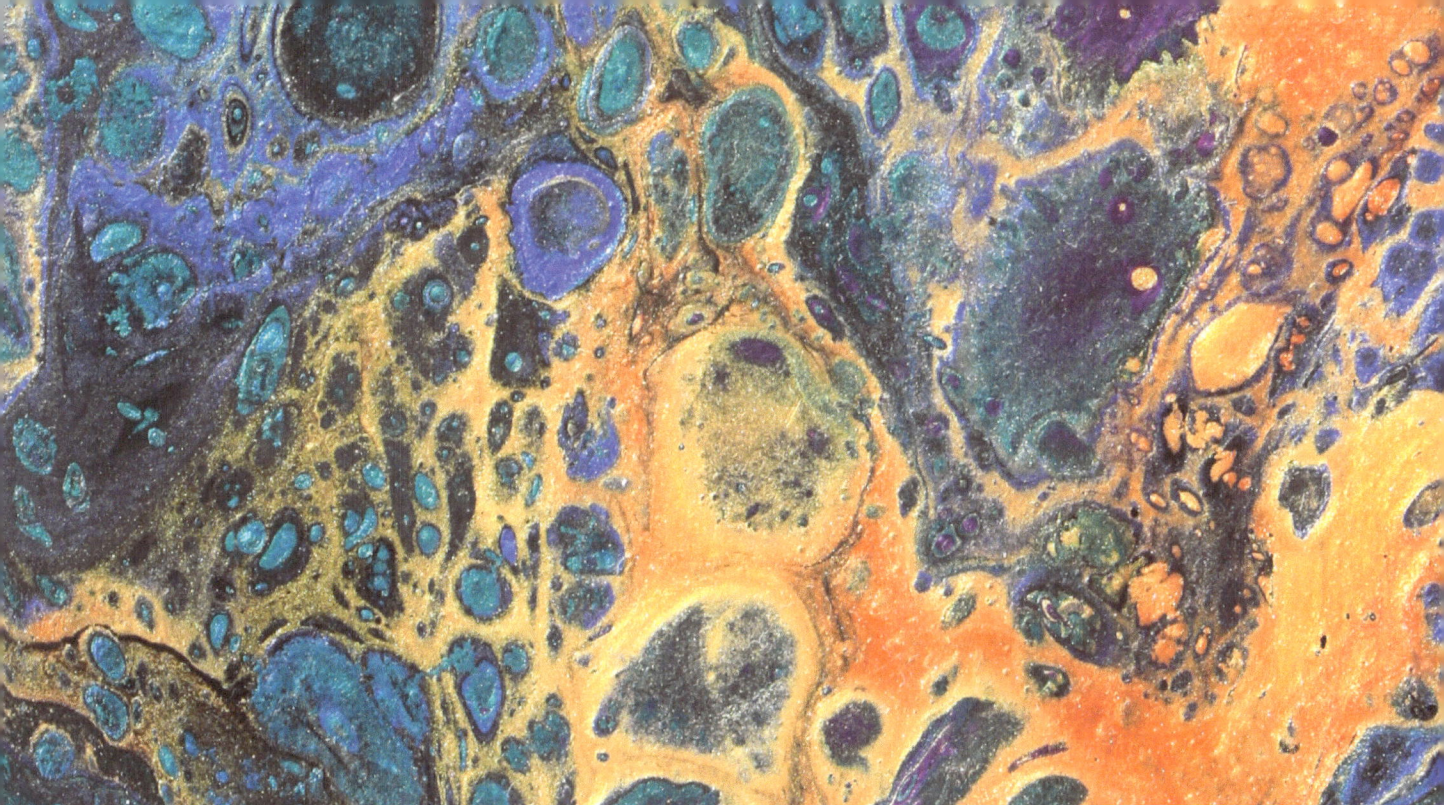

GOLD GREEN by Mihaela Berg Divald

Loud Music

I turn the music up
Hoping that the melody
Like a blanket
Covers the long-last
Traces of pain
That resides in me

—Louise Roberts

Letting Go

No amount of guilt pouring my way,
Will change the way I feel.
You can try again and again,
False victory is not real.

My peace is a precious gift,
Soul on fire eternal goal,
Restless world,
Feelings stretched,
Light will lead the way of letting go!

—Tihana Šiletić

Happy Sadness

I'm still injured
And broken inside.
You'd never notice it, though
I laugh aloud all the time.
No one would ever imagine
All the tears that I've cried,
No one would ever notice
The pain that's hidden
Behind my smile.
In order to protect ourselves and
Avoid all sort of judgement
We learn how to lie.
If people had empathy and
Never ever betrayed us
We'd have no need to hide.
Will society learn this lesson
Or will we have to fake
Until the last day
Of our lives?

—Yara Artiles

Melody

A sugar pill to bide the time
Between surcease and pain.
A pharmaceutical rosary,
Each bead prescribed in vain.
Swallow on an empty stomach,
Before you sleep and when you wake.
Or turn the music way up loud,
No better pill to take.
Placebos sit in plastic jars,
The hopes of science all in line.
I do not know their names by heart,
But oh this song…remembers mine.

—Margarita Martinez

Love's Screaming

Winding down the paths
Twisting and turning
Yearning
For something never had
The touch you can't feel
The smell of your skin
Love's screaming
Whispering of words
Never said.
I catch my breath
In your voice
Lost in serenity
Love holds me
Still in the tranquility
Of space and time
I let go
Standing on the white line
Some souls build a home
In your veins
And they come and go
With every beat of your heart.

—Alicia Lewis

My Strength

Loved you from the moment I saw your eyes,
Standing on the corner as you
Passed me by,
Drawn by magic into you
With all my heart
I can't stand to be one day
   from you apart
Please don't let my anger
Change me into who I'm not
I have this feeling in me
For much too long,
How can I explain something
I don't understand
Stuck in a pond of mud
I can't move an inch away.

Weight of love I gave you
Is much more than you can take
You know all my weaknesses
But you don't know you are my strength.

I drag you into my world
I painted black and blue
All my troubles, doubts, and fears came true and reflected on you.
If I could release you from this pain
I would
I don't know how to let you go
Even I know I should.

Weight of love I gave you
Is much more than you can take
You know all my weaknesses
But you don't know you are my strength.

—Mihaela Berg Divald

INNER LIGHT by Mel Eatherington

Eons in the Making

Enjoy the moments even the ones where the sidewalk ends
They slip through our fingers like people's actions, schoolgirl crushes
What happened between the first kiss and the last flicker of the flame?
It is a pilgrimage and forbearance from spite to Grace
Eons in the making of the space between two planets
Tangled in gravity
Destined to collide in the heavens and stars

—Darla Dallas

Skipping Act Two

Do we really have to play act two?
Too many obstacles
The only way through
Party of a lifetime

Invite the masses
Only the passionate stay
Ostentatious survive in these places
Not likely me

Gone with a twinkle of stars
Wind on my face
Life made it real
My party of a lifetime

—Darla Dallas

Desperate and Divine

Desperate and Divine
It's a tug of war
Two words on the line
One is hopeless
Reaching out
For that something we can't have
The other is
A taste of something sweet
That runs and bursts through your veins
You grasp the one to hold
Onto forever
But to get it
You need the other.

Desperate and Divine
In the quiet
Two words on the line
Connected and conflicting
Let go hold on
Forever entangled
Forever apart
Between the two
There's light and dark
You grasp the one to hold
Onto forever
But to get it
You need the other.

—Alicia Lewis

Hearts Beat

Marching to a drummer
Hands unseen
Steering us together
Winds unseen
Filling up our sails
Driven by the weather
Lost control
Forces of our nature
Come along
Following the Piper
Down the path
Marching it together
Where we stand
Do we face each other
Where we stand
Walking hand in hand
Can we stay
Or will we turn away
Will we stand
And face the storm together
Or will we run
Turn and run for cover
Who are we
What's it all mean
Hand in hand
Standing in the storm
Hearts beat
Marching to the drummer…

—Jack William Finley

COLOR OF MUSIC by Andrea Worley

REACHING OUT TO YOU by Lizzie Ottaway

Heart, Spirit, Soul

Parts of me
Never had learned, how to make them whole
Words cut so deep
Heart can't handle the storm
After it's gone, it's peace and quiet
I'm left all alone
With my thoughts
Rain of tears
Amount of fears
Emptiness inside me
Can't fill the cup of joy
You play cruel with me
I feel like a broken toy…

—Mihaela Berg Divald

Iuno

Whispering silence, voices in my head.
I can remember everything you said.
But it is all
Only in my head.

Lightning, roaring thunder, hail,
My head is aching.
All I can think is:
Stop it, stop it. Stop it in some way!

Rain on the window, the air is grey,
My heart is aching.
All I can feel is:
Fear—oh, go away!

—Jana Wiebach

Alone in the night
the music sings to me
Alone in the night
the music comforts me
Alone in the night
the music teaches me
Alone in the night
the music helps me see
Alone in the night
the music brings me dreams
Alone in the night
the music brings me hope
Alone in the night
the music brings faith
Alone in the night
the music brings peace
Alone in the night
the night restores me
Alone in the night
I am music
I am free

All of these people
Frolic in the sun.
Light and heat
Worshiping the Sun.
Watching from the distance
These are not my people
This is not my tribe
I thrive upon the moonlight
Dancing through puddles
In the rain
Clouds in my skies
Thunder in the distance
lightning lights my eyes
A night blooming flower
Moonlight dreams
Starlight fantasies
Dancing through puddles in the rain

—Jack William Finley

Back To Earth

when the silence of deep space
became deafening it was finally
time to risk the danger
the fiery business of falling

back to earth, falling
back to earth

had a rough landing
struggled again at learning
how to submit successfully
to the laws of gravity, falling

back to earth, falling
back to earth

flirting with overwhelm trading
weightlessness for sand between my toes walking
along the beach the sound of waves breaking, dogs barking
replacing the cool rhythmic humming of machines purring
and one single heartbeat beating, falling

back to earth falling
back to earth

trading the cold eternal night
where no one can hear you scream
for sweet little whispers when waking
to the scents of fresh bread baking
and cool salty sea breezes sneaking
in through the window warming
us in the bright sun shining
glad we risked the danger
the fiery business of falling

back to earth, falling
back to earth falling
back to earth

—Carell Casey

You and me
A poppy field
Tea
Apple pie
Clouds reflected
In your eyes.

Sunset
Soft breeze
Music
Kisses
Birds in the sky
Your smile.

A sweet dream in July.

—Camila Alvarez

life

unfurling
unfolding
unrolling
like fern leaves
like rosebuds
like waves
our lives spiral
onward and upward
then curl back down
to earth
each time we try
we climb higher
than ever dared before
though our view
keeps expanding
tomorrow
stays hidden
like a galaxy
unknown

—erica dirven

When you hold me
I can feel
The flowers blooming
Inside my chest

A natural effect
Conceived by
Your alluring
Light

—Louise Roberts

I Lost Sight

If I wrote a book
It wouldn't take long
For the world to know
My heart doesn't know
Where it belongs

There was a time
When I knew
What my mind's
Thoughts
Meant

And somehow
In all of this confusion
I lost sight
Of all of the
Important things

Like when you
Were there to
Hold me
I felt like I could do anything

And now when
Another soul comforts me
It doesn't
Quite feel the same

Yet somehow I know
When I'm looking at the moon
I can feel you
My heart says so many things

And you will
Never hear them
Because the fates
Moved us towards different pathways.

—Sonia Vance

For M.O. Thank You

I wanted to re-read
Mary's poems
In light of her death
And then I remembered
They are all packed in a box
Marked y's books
My books
My special books

Poetry and nonfiction and fiction
Dry books of theory and ethics
Light books for fun and sunny days
Long literate books coaxing me into another world
Reminding me that others have inhabited this dimension
Short inspirational books of wisdom, reverential musings
And sightings of the sameness of us all
No matter what we look like or smell like or like to eat
Novels of current times past times of worlds never existing
That bring me to my knees in fury and laughter and longing for another
World so like the one in my mind

In those boxes Mary's poetry is carefully packed
Until I am able to place her back on the bookshelf
Where I have the privilege to take them down, to re-read to cry to smile
to laugh and to wonder how it was that she could say all the things my
heart has wanted to say
And how well she says these things and how well I hear them

— yk miyazaki

Saturday 8pm BST

At the start of a single day
My hands hold many smooth pebbles
After dreamless sleep
I skim them into a raggedy future
Absent kisses, ungiven hugs
I got gussied up
You could still be the best thing
Choices I've made
I look at you and a different me reflects
Nostalgia

—Lizzie Ottaway

REWORKED by Denise Denevi

Curious Collaboration

In my closet
I lay in prostration
The weight of Holy Days on my back

Listening hard to the conversations of my rowdy shoes
They are keeping the story alive

I sit, naming all my parts
I choose each word, writing down the days
Home is not these four walls
Remind me of this later

As we are defining a new normal
Composing a new definition of hope
Nature continues in Divine Splendor
Offering no apology
Keep turning towards that light
Remember those echoes of laughter
Those leaves like clapping hands

This is where we begin
Cracking the spine of the book
Poetic jumpstart
Silhouette of wings, just before the leap

Your face leaning in
Together is not the same
Halfway is still too far
Your face, the chords of a song F, A, C, E
There is a symphony in those eyes
And I am relearning my lines
Choking on these words
You are my grace
You are my mercy
This dancing fire
Ember of hope

I am playing the song of you with sore fingers

—Vanessa Power

A Different World

You and me in a different world
I want to wake up from a great night's sleep
Freedom from the weight of the world's grief and incompetence
A common flirt with a guy
Sit in a café
Excited to make plans with a friend
Our kindness flows both ways
It helps my kids
My small world
My selfish dreams combat regrets
Will you be here when I need you?
Emotions will pass, Emotions will heal
Our kindness flows both ways
Tune your guitar to the minor chords of possibilities
Dream to leap for joy!
Change ready for something good right now
Ready for safety in song

—Darla Dallas

GLIMPSE by Cindy O.

lightbody

what if we'd lost this body of light
how we lost scott hutchison
or chris cornell
his melodies, empathy
the joke and then the laugh

what if i'd been lost
to the dead of dublin's night
the july i lay paralyzed
while my feet pursued reprieve
through dark, capricious streets

it is april before we know
my fingers hovering over dial tones
my fingers gouging wounds
        his voice
            a beacon

don't give in

it will be april before we know

—courtney lavender

BOOKSHELF by Anna Lvova

One More Time Together

I sit in the silence
Somewhere between real and imagined
Your words lost in my mind
With hope where your last thought was left

I can feel your words
As they shout out in the wind
Blowing gently in the breeze of time
Held in ethereal beauty of being

The quiet in my mind
Reminds me of your kindness
And that through all of this
The next chapter is yet to be written

—MK Brennan

The Last Page of the Book

And we're starting…now.

How can I
Given a certain time
Given all the time in the world
Tell you
What the last five months have meant to me
How he changed my life
Saved my life
Saved us all
Created a blanket fort in the chat beneath his smile
A family that nursed me through sickness
Watched me be reborn
Again
A family I cannot lose, will not lose
Don't want to lose
Songs
The flame that drew us
The glue that bonded us
Now tangible
Made us powerful enough to help others
United, unmeltable
Except by his fire
And this world
Still burning
Always burning
Always

—Alethea Kontis

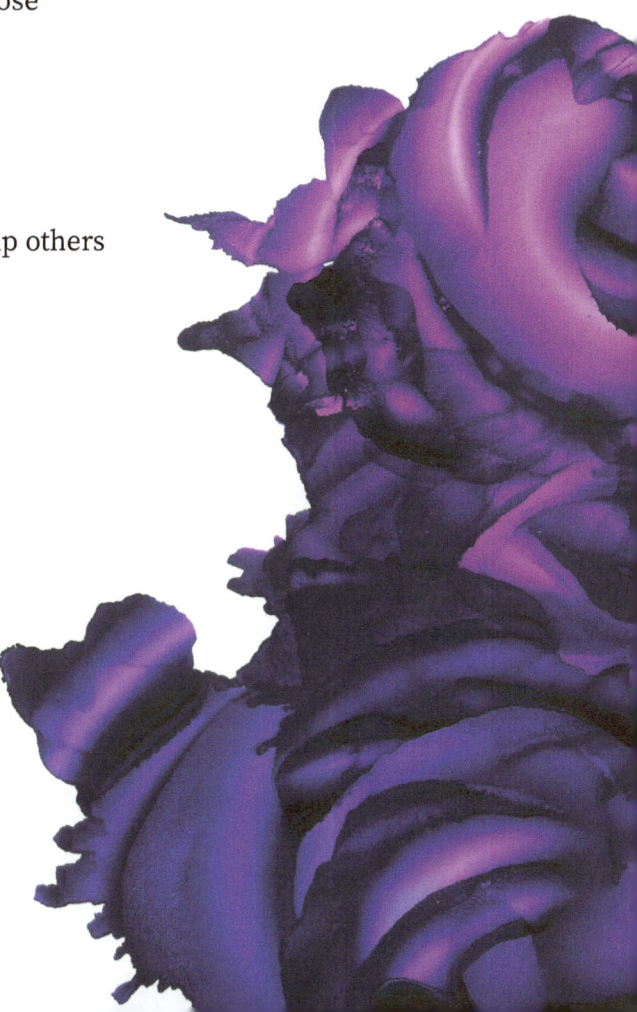

ROSE SPECTACULAR by Mel Eatherington

AGA RZYMSKA

What is your Instagram handle?

@aga.rz

Where are you from originally?

Poland

Where do you live now?

London, UK

What is your occupation?

Self-employed

What are your hobbies?

I love to draw—trying to do this as often as I can. I love music and go to a lot of gigs (not now, sadly), travel a bit, and read in my spare time.

When did you first join Songwrite?

I joined the livestreams and Saturday Songwrite from the first day.

What songs are your lyrics in?

None

What's your favorite SP song of all time?

My favourite Snow Patrol songs are "Run" and "Life on Earth" (can't choose one)

What's your favorite SP song for 2020?

I really like "Reaching Out to You" from the new EP.

What's your Saturday Songwrite story?

Snow Patrol have been one of my all-time favourite bands for almost 20 years. I lived in not a very big town in Poland, and I had no chance to see them live for a very long time. So when I moved to London and started my "gigs life," Snow Patrol was very high on the "bands to see" list. They are great live—I've seen them already three times and can't wait for this madness to end and the gigs to come back! The lockdown livestreams, thanks to Gary, made me feel like Snow Patrol is not just a band. We actually can connect, even do something together, and that's amazing. I live on my own and feel good about that, but when you're at home 24/7 things like the livestreams can do miracles really, and I even haven't felt lonely too much because of this.

Is there anything else that you would like to add about yourself?

I like hands. I think they can often tell us more than words and I draw them very often.

ALETHEA KONTIS

What is your Instagram handle?
>@aletheakontis

Where are you from originally?
>Burlington, Vermont, USA

Where do you live now?
>Space Coast, Florida, USA

What is your occupation?
>Author

What are your hobbies?
>Storm Chasing, Chaos Gardening, Fishing with Dad, Learning Languages, Playing Guitar Badly

When did you first join Songwrite?
>Week 4

What songs are your lyrics in?
>Week 5 - "On the Edge of All This" - upside-down (became "upside-downness")
>
>Week 7a - nightmare
>
>Week 9 - everyday magic (became "magic")
>
>Week 11 - Not a damn word (yup, that was me)

What's your favorite SP song of all time?
>"The Lightning Strike" (the entire 16-minute opus)

What's your favorite SP song for 2020?
>"Empress"

Did you submit artwork for the EP cover contest?
>No, I was on deadline. (I titled the novella I wrote "On the Edge of All This" in honor of *The Fireside Sessions* EP)

What's your Saturday Songwrite story?
>Okay. So here's the infamous Songwrite Week 11 story.
>
>The week of May 25th was a tough one, full of protests and riots that shook the world. Gary reminded us that Songwrite was a safe space; we should dig deep and be honest with our lyrics. I attended that early summer day from a blanket by the pond, my front-row seat to the historic manned rocket launch. I left Instagram only long enough to record SpaceX ferrying Doug and Bob into the stratosphere. The air around me was still rumbling when I signed back into Songwrite to find that Gary had turned his camera to the television. He and the Songwriters were watching the launch, too. It felt like all my new friends were sitting right there by the pond

ALETHEA KONTIS   (CONTINUED)

with me. Pure magic.

Then we got back to Songwrite work. Lyrics time. I typed words and phrases into the chat, one after another. And another. And another. And another. Gary saw none of them. When he filled four pages of his pad with our suggestions he called an end to the session. I had contributed nothing. So I typed, "Not a damn word. ACK!" into the chat. At least my Songwrite friends would laugh.

Of course, Gary saw *that*.

"'Not a damn word, ack?' Go on, then. Give me your best stuff. I'll wait. I'll wait. I'll wait. I'll wait. I promise I'll wait."

I might have had a minor heart attack. That comment wasn't even meant for Gary! But he had seen it...and now he was talking to me. I needed only to answer. So I typed. And I typed. Nothing got through. It was like trying to shout through a brick wall. I kept at it for what felt like hours. Days. Did he even remember my name at this point? Eventually I just started typing "pandemonium" over and over. ("Pandemonium" was *not* my best stuff.)

Gary saw none of it. But he kept waiting. For me. He thought I had become suddenly shy for being put on the spot (Ha!) and said gently encouraging things. He expressed sympathy for all of the Songwriters whose lyrics never made it into songs but who continued to join in week after week. He kept talking, and I kept typing. Nothing.

Eventually, some sweet Songwriter suggested that Gary just use "not a damn word" as my lyric suggestion. Gary commended that lovely advice, scribbled the words down, and signed off to compose the song.

Flushed and frustrated (and knowing Gary would be away for an hour), I went live on my own Instagram account to tell my side of the story. Camila and a few other Songwriters checked in. It felt so good to speak and actually be heard.

When Gary returned to present us with yet another gorgeous song cobbled out of our chaos, he read off the list of lyrics he'd used. When he got to "not a damn word," the chat erupted with friends cheering my name. (They even spelled it right!) Pretty sure my heart exploded into butterflies right then. I might have cried. These beautiful Songwriters from all over the world *cared* about me and what happened in my story.

That meant so much to me. It still does.

When Evelyn posted the art she drew for Week 11's song, I made it my desktop wallpaper. And when Gary didn't go live on Instagram the following Saturday, I went live in his honor, so that any wayward Songwriter might have a safe place to commiserate. I wanted to express my heartfelt gratitude for their presence in Gary's chat, and in my life.

I went live the next Saturday, too, since Gary wasn't around. And the next. And the Saturday after that. I jokingly referred to myself as "The Last Songwriter" since mine had been the last lyric Gary wrote

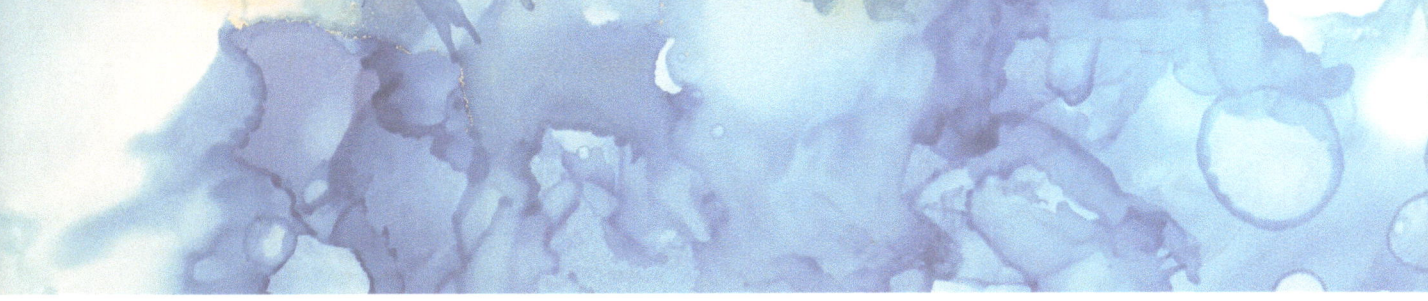

down before his extended absence, and I tried not to feel completely horrible about that fact. I called our meetings "Saturday Songwriters Not-So-Anonymous" and then just "SSW Chat." I drew a roaring fire on a giant piece of paper and taped it to my bookshelf. I found a little stuffed polar bear in a bunch of old things—I named him Gary Jr. and brought him online as my co-host. Somewhere in the middle of all that (and definitely inspired by Evelyn and MK) the idea for this book was born.

And then Week 12 of SSW Chat coincided with Week 12 of Actual Saturday Songwrite. How's that for synchronicity? I went live while Gary was off composing—it worked out perfectly. I was no longer The Last Songwriter, and [*fingers crossed*] that would not be our last song.

The SSW Chats still happen on my Instagram every Saturday at "Gary O'Clock," and hopefully will still be happening by the time you read this lovely little book we made to celebrate ourselves. Consider yourselves officially invited.

Is there anything else that you would like to add about yourself?

I love my Songwrite family with all my heart. It's so odd to think that once upon a time we might have never met! It has been a joy to see this community grow and bond across spaces both virtual and real. I am truly honored to be a cog in this machine of perpetual light.

ALICIA LEWIS

What is your Instagram handle?
> @Vanillamoon777

Where are you from originally?
> California, USA

Where do you live now?
> Oregon, USA

What is your occupation?
> Preschool teacher, but now a stay-at-home mom

What are your hobbies?
> Reading, crafting, gardening, nature hikes

When did you first join Songwrite?
> At the very beginning

What songs are your lyrics in?
> "The Curve Of Earth" (Unforgotten) and "Light Years" (Incandescent)

What's your favorite SP song of all time?
> "It's Beginning To Get To Me," "Make This Go On Forever," and "This Isn't Everything You Are" (Honestly I have way too many and can't choose but these three will ALWAYS be on my list!)

What's your favorite SP song for 2020?
> "Empress"

What's your Saturday Songwrite story?
> Gary saved my sanity during the lockdown. Saturday Songwrite was an exciting and engaging experience for me to look forward to each week. It sparked my creativity in a way, to come up with lyric ideas. It also brought me closer to our SP family!

Is there anything else that you would like to add about yourself?
> I love cats, music, nature, and books! I am vegan, and I try my best to live eco friendly.

ANDREA WORLEY

What is your Instagram handle?
    @Drea19704981

Where are you from originally?
    California, USA

Where do you live now?
    Colorado, USA

What is your occupation?
    CNA, RMA

What are your hobbies?
    painting, crafts, poetry, writing and photography.

When did you first join Songwrite?
    I started SSW with the very first one and finished with that last one!

What songs are your lyrics in?
    Week 5 - "On the Edge of All This" - We'll meet again

What's your favorite SP song of all time?
    "Just Say Yes"

MAN ON MOON by Andrea Worley

ANNA LVOVA

What is your Instagram handle?

@anna.lvova

Where are you from originally?

Saint Petersburg, Russia

Where do you live now?

Saint Petersburg, Russia

What is your occupation?

Writer, artist, illustrator

What are your hobbies?

Drawing, writing

When did you first join Songwrite?

I watched all SSW sessions.

What songs are your lyrics in?

None. Gary wrote down one of my phrases (Suffering happiness), but it wasn't used in the lyrics.

What's your favorite SP song of all time?

"Run"

What's your favorite SP song for 2020?

The songs from Week 7 (second one) and week 10 of SSW.

What's your Saturday Songwrite story?

Gary and his music have always been a powerful source of inspiration for me, that's why being a part of the creative process is a special and precious experience. I'm infinitely grateful to Gary for having let me into this space, so to say. In a daze after the first few sessions, I drew Gary, merging live gigs and Saturday Songwrite sessions into one drawing. I had the audacity to suggest it for the cover—just as an idea—but Gary was so unbelievably sweet that he included it in the booklet! SSW will forever have a special place in my heart as something that brought me not only happiness, but also so many friends all over the world.

CAMILA ALVAREZ

What is your Instagram handle?

@camila_alvarez_sp / @snowpatrolnewsbr

Where are you from originally?

Curitiba, Brazil

Where do you live now?

Londrina, Brazil

What is your occupation?

Secretary / Psychology student

What are your hobbies?

Music, movies, volleyball, literature

When did you first join Songwrite?

The first live session.

What songs are your lyrics in? (If any)

I have words in songs 3 and 4.

What's your favorite SP song of all time?

"Set The Fire To The Third Bar"

What's your favorite SP song for 2020?

"Life On Earth"

What's your Saturday Songwrite story?

I'm a big fan of the band, and I was already watching Gary in the other lives. So when he started doing the Saturday sessions, I watched too. Was a great and unusual idea he had, and even not knowing any chords and not being great at english and writing, I did my best to be part of it. Was not only great to see him working, but spending time with him was also amazing. We know he is a genius, but making different melodies and putting all together, in a short time, was impressive. Not only that, but all the lyrics that people sent, being on a song or not, were impressive too. And use the songs, that been amazingly recorded by Snow Patrol and friends, to make an EP, and help people in need, it's the cherry on top (of a great tiramisu).

Is there anything else that you would like to add about yourself?

I have the 'Snow Patrol News BR' Instagram. I created this "group" in 2010 on Twitter, and wasn't able to update in the last years. But I started the page again on Instagram last year, where I try to update fans about the band news. It's also a great way to chat with the friends, that I've made through the lives, from different places of the world. Friends that are talented and kind, and are always there, when involves the band or not. Gary made a weird year better, made us admire him more, and also create a family.

CARELL CASEY

What is your Instagram handle?

> @carell.casey

Where are you from originally?

> Wisconsin, USA

When did you first join Songwrite?

> I watched most or all of the Saturday Songwrites live.

What songs are your lyrics in? (If any)

> None

What's your favorite SP song of all time?

> That's a hard question! I'm going to go with "Set the Fire to the Third Bar"

What's your favorite SP song for 2020?

> From Wildness I really like the groove in "Dark Switch." Also some of the lyrics remind me of a poem I wrote once. And some of the imagery in the video remind me of a dream I had once.

What's your Saturday Songwrite story?

> I have been a casual Snow Patrol fan since 2006 when I heard "Chasing Cars" on the radio in New Zealand when I was there traveling.

CINDY O.

What is your Instagram handle?
@cindyswissmiss

Where are you from originally?
Switzerland

Where do you live now?
Switzerland

What is your occupation?
Teacher, but I'm also an archaeologist at heart

What are your hobbies?
Photography, travelling, picked up my guitar again

When did you first join Songwrite?
Week 2, but couldn't contribute until week 4 because of technical issues

What songs are your lyrics in?
"Light Years"—somebody repeated what I wrote and that made it into the song.

What's your favorite SP song of all time?
I cannot choose

What's your favorite SP song for 2020?
"The Curve of Earth"

What's your Saturday Songwrite story?
I pretty much stumbled into it, and I'm so glad I did. I have become a lot more creative again, trying out different things with words and music and I have made so many new friends all over the world.

CORINA OLIVER

What is your Instagram handle?

@ corinaol

Where are you from originally?

Argentina

Where do you live now?

Buenos Aires, Argentina

What is your occupation?

I'm an architect.

What are your hobbies?

I have loved music since I was little and I love to sing. That is why I decided to start studying singing 11 years ago. When, sometimes, inspiration touches me, I also paint.

When did you first join Songwrite?

I joined SSW the first time Gary did it.

What songs are your lyrics in?

Unfortunately the algorithm didn't show my words on Gary's screen so I have no lyrics in the songs!

What's your favorite SP song of all time?

Although there are many songs that I love on Snow Patrol, my favorite is still "Called Out in the Dark", because it brings back many memories of a beautiful time.

What's your favorite SP song for 2020?

"Don't Give In" has been my favorite since the release of Wildness.

Did you submit artwork for the EP cover contest?

I submitted my artwork for the EP cover contest. I tried to express myself through the tools that I know, the paint, and the design programs that I use in my profession. At first I believed that I could not do anything similar to what others did. All the people were being very creative, even before the contest was released. But when I was given the option to email it, I did.

What's your Saturday Songwrite story?

In March I lost my job as a result of the many problems that Covid-19 brought. Normally, during the hours that Gary did live shows on Instagram, I would be in the office working. So I was able to be there for the daily songs he did during the month of March, and I was there when he announced the Saturday Songwriters. Of course I was there!

Is there anything else that you would like to add about yourself?

> I tried to write when the idea for the book came up on Alethea's live Instagram, when Gary paused. (I'm so glad Alethea took the SSW's torch!) I never wrote poetry in my life. I did not try to be original or do it well, I just wanted to express what I felt and thought in those moments.
>
> This was an absolutely incredible experience for me, as I know it was for many of us. I have no words that have not been said over and over again during this time. In each of you I have found words that represent what I feel.
>
> I am eternally grateful to Gary in particular, but each and every day I am really happy for the beautiful people I met because of this.

COURTNEY LAVENDER

What is your Instagram handle?

@xsandarrows

Where are you from originally?

Los Angeles, California, USA

Where do you live now?

Los Angeles, California, USA

What is your occupation?

I work in the music industry

What are your hobbies?

Music, Writing, Traveling, Hiking in the San Gabriel Mountains

When did you first join Songwrite?

I attended every songwrite, starting with the first one.

What songs are your lyrics in?

"Light Years" uses the word "birdsong" which I contributed, though it was someone else who said it a few minutes after I did whose comment Gary actually saw.

What's your favorite SP song of all time?

"The Symphony"

What's your favorite SP song for 2020?

"On the Edge Of All This"

What's your Saturday Songwrite story?

I was initially excited just to be part of the creation of a song, to "hang out" with Gary and watch his process. As a songwriter, I was very curious how it would go. I didn't expect to make friends and so quickly feel a part of a true community. A friend joked with me that I should write a song using words and phrases contributed during the sessions that Gary didn't use, and when I left a comment on one of the Snow Patrol Instagram posts saying so, I met two people who immediately turned this notion into a writing community, and eventually, this book.

Is there anything else that you would like to add about yourself?

I have a band called Xs & ARROWs, for which I write, sing, and play guitar and other occasional instruments. We have an EP out on all platforms called *From Here* and will be recording new songs as soon as the fates allow. I have been writing poetry for years, and have been published in *The Honest Ulsterman*, *Bangor Literary Journal*, *Picaroon Poetry*, *Altadena Poetry Review*, and others. I have put together two handmade chapbooks and hope one day to have a poetry collection officially published.

DARLA DALLAS

What is your Instagram handle?
> @darladallas

Where are you from originally?
> Beeville, Texas, USA

Where do you live now?
> Fort Worth, Texas, USA

What is your occupation?
> Construction Project Estimator

What are your hobbies?
> Portrait and Event Photography, Poetry, Songwriting

When did you first join Songwrite?
> From the first Saturday to the last

What songs are your lyrics in?
> I wished my lyrics suggestions would be used in some way either directly or in spirit. The only words Gary wrote down of mine that I noticed were "you're cute when you're funny" (or was it "you're funny when you're cute"). It's sad because I can't remember. I think that was Week 4, which is one of my favorite songs—I call it "Silver Linings." My flirty words were not used in the song, but it was fun to show up every week to contribute suggestions.

What's your favorite SP song of all time?
> "Just Say Yes"

What's your favorite SP song for 2020?
> "Empress" (reworked version) And SSW Week 4 ("Silver Linings")

What's your Saturday Songwrite story?
> There was serendipity involved when Gary Lightbody offered to write songs together on Instagram live. I joined him every Saturday. Attempting to write songs for fun was a great journey of divine shenanigans. One of my top values is creativity and music. I made a new goal to start writing lyrics and poetry a few weeks before we started the Saturday Songwriting sessions. I had no idea how to get there without the music, but I know what I want to do with my time and attention. The miracle of perfect timing and kindness gave me a safe place to explore these goals. I've learned so much about songwriting and the creative process. I will continue my journey of writing with a new perspective of hope and anticipation. Thank you, Gary, for the music and the kindness. You are a blessing.

Is there anything else that you would like to add about yourself?
> I've always wanted to be a part of the hero's journey. I dreamed it would be as an extra in a movie or TV show. This is much better than that dream. A real beautiful journey with a purpose to help people. I'm so grateful for each and every one of the Saturday Songwriters.

DEBORAH THACKRAY

What is your Instagram handle?
> @Debiathackers

Where are you from originally?
> Hull, England (but lived in London for 17 years!)

Where do you live now?
> Beverley, East Yorkshire, UK

What is your occupation?
> Safeguarding/Child Protection Officer

What are your hobbies?
> Music, theatre, walking, baking and socializing with friends.

When did you first join Songwrite?
> Week 1

What songs are your lyrics in?
> None, but I tried very hard!!

What's your favorite SP song of all time?
> "Don't Give In"

What's your favorite SP song for 2020?
> All from *The Fireside Sessions* EP

What's your Saturday Songwrite story?
> In 2004 I walked into a pub with my friend and the song "Run" was on. I said "I love this song," and then I looked up and the video was playing on the screen. I remember saying "the singer's not bad either"—that was the beginning of my love affair with Snow Patrol! Never in my wildest dreams did I think I would be spending my Saturday and Thursday nights (plus the odd bonus night) in the company of this gorgeous man (albeit virtually)! Lockdown was a difficult time, as I don't have any family, and I couldn't see my friends. To be able to be part of Saturday Songwrite was an amazing experience that helped me get through it. I will be forever grateful for all the happy memories during such a difficult time. It's been lovely seeing people around the world unite and create an amazing EP. I still cry when I listen to it! Although it is over, I have made contact with some lovely people and hopefully one day we will be able to meet in person!

Is there anything else that you would like to add about yourself?
> I'm a happy-go-lucky person who has overcome lots of challenges but still here to tell the story!!!!!!!
>
> Saturday Songwriters and Gary Lightbody and everyone involved—you rock! Thank you for making lockdown so bearable. Saturday nights won't be the same!!! Take care everyone.

DENISE SHAFER DENEVI

What is your Instagram handle?
> @denise.denevi

Where are you from originally?
> California, USA

Where do you live now?
> Kansas City, Missouri, USA

When did you first join Songwrite?
> April 11, 2020 (Week 4)

What songs are your lyrics in?
> Week 5 - "On the Edge of All This" - falling down
>
> Week 9 - Leave the light on one more time (Gary added "for me")

What's your favorite SP song of all time?
> "Just Say Yes"

What's your favorite SP song for 2020?
> "The Curve of Earth"

What's your Saturday Songwrite story?
> I live alone in the Midwest. Kansas City, Missouri, to be exact. I fill my spaces with things that make me smile, like shells from the sea and photos of my family. My space is bright with hues of greens and blues to help remind me of the ocean. I am a California girl at heart, born and raised on the West Coast. My journey landed me here in the Midwest many moons ago, and it is here in the Midwest where my treasure grows: my grandchildren. I often define myself by the work I do, but this is not who I am; it is just what I do, many hours a day, many days a week. I am a Board Certified Behavior Analyst, implementing the principles of Applied Behavior Analysis as a way to change behavior. So, in 2020 when Covid-19 invaded our planet, I like many others, spent many days working from home.
>
> Feeling especially alone one Saturday (isolated from my grandchildren, my big birthday vacation plans cancelled), I was scrolling through my Facebook account and who should appear live and bantering with fans, but Gary Lightbody. What?! Gary from Snow Patrol—Live!! Yes, indeed there he was, and he kept putting his hand to his mouth and gesturing for fans to come over to Insta for his Saturday Songwrite. What? Insta? Insta what? Instagram? But I don't have Instagram.
>
> So, as soon as he signed off Facebook, I went to my Apple Store app and downloaded Instagram. I fumbled my way through and managed to "follow" Gary Lightbody and Snow Patrol. And, well, my life as I

DENISE SHAFER DENEVI (CONTINUED)

knew it would never be the same. I became a Saturday Songwriter.

It didn't take long for the experience to begin transforming my life. I began to feel a part of something intimately magical. There were times when Gary responded directly to my comments, and he even wrote down some of my lyric suggestions. Bits and pieces found their way into the songs, and then one seven-word lyric made it all the way into one of the songs! I was overjoyed—to the moon and back. Wanting others to share in that joy, I slowed down on my commenting, hoping others would get words in.

That is the way it became with the Songwriters, a spirit of togetherness and love for one another. It resonated throughout our sessions. With humor, and banter, and love. We inspired one another in such a wondrous way. The art, the music, the poetry and the friendships that have manifested as a result of one man's altruistic love of music and humanity, is a testament to the power of such love.

ERICA DIRVEN

What is your Instagram handle?

@hozho67

Where are you from originally? / Where do you live now?

I am from the Netherlands. I live in a small, old town called Haarlem. I was born there too. It is very close to our nation's capital city, Amsterdam.

What is your occupation?

I almost became a lawyer but changed direction when I was near the end of my studies. It proved to be one of the best choices I ever made, because I absolutely love what I do now. I am a Montessori teacher.

For almost twenty years I have been the Head Teacher of a bilingual Montessori preschool in the centre of Amsterdam, with children and staff from all over the globe. The average amount of different home languages spoken in our classroom is fourteen! A lot of children are even brand new to the country when they come to the school—by "brand new," I mean they are still staying in a hotel waiting for a proper house.

What are your hobbies?

Listening to music, reading, going to the cinema once or twice a week to see mainly arthouse films (but I also love a good Marvel/ Star Wars, etc. blockbuster), hunting for vintage clothes and shoes, collecting Art Nouveau/Art Deco/Arts & Crafts objects and jewellery (I love Pablo's house!) and going for walks. I am a true introvert

When did you first join Songwrite?

I missed the very first one and only dared to watch during the second one. I actively joined on number three and fanatically took part in all the ones that followed.

What songs are your lyrics in?

I finally, finally got some lyrics written down in Week 10. Gary wrote down:

- diving deep into your wave

- lighthouse

- a wave on the tide of you

The last one made it into the song!

(And because of Alethea's video I am no longer upset about all the other ones that he probably never even saw…)

What's your favorite SP song of all time?

I love many, but here I will have to name the song that pulled me in deep, so much deeper than ever before: "What If This is All the Love You Ever Get." The first time I heard it, I started to cry almost uncontrollably. It still gives me the chills every time I hear it. That whole album got me hooked for life. Every single song resonates with me.

What's your favorite SP song for 2020?

Our song "Reaching Out to You!"

What's your Saturday Songwrite story?

During lockdown, I accidentally stumbled

ERICA DIRVEN (CONTINUED)

upon a Thursday live by Gary. I loved every single bit about that! And then he announced the Saturday Songwrite sessions. I tuned in and was hooked. He did not write any of my words down, but I did not mind, because I was not sure about them anyway and I loved the energy of the group. I loved being connected with the globe and being busy with two of my favourite things in life: words and music.

I started gathering words and phrases throughout the weeks that followed and started thinking of ways to get him to write my words down. I had a whole list of tactics in my head. And the words were gradually getting better, so I got a bit frustrated (again thank you so much, Alethea, for your "Not A Damn Word" video. It saved my sanity!).

I was getting more confident about what I was writing. And then he actually wrote something down! He spoke my words! They ended up in a song I love. It is the one with the brilliant "Johnny Cash and June" line (Week 10), and I really hope it will get finished properly one day.

The moment he wrote my words and spoke them were my highlight of the sessions. It felt like winning the lottery. I actually did a little happy dance in my living room.

And then we watched the launch together on the last one... It was such a strangely sad and emotional day and week. I miss us!

But this is what Saturday Songwrite has given me:

Writing confidence

Loads of lovely new friends (hopefully for life!)

A feeling of togetherness

Hope for the future

Loads of Garyisms floating around my head at all times, making me grin whenever they pop up.

Is there anything else that you would like to add about yourself?

A little bit about my instagram name:

Hozho, or rather hózhó (pronounced something like hoezjoe) is a Navajo concept that means "to walk in beauty." It refers to the interconnectedness between beauty, harmony, and goodness in all things physical and spiritual that results in health and well-being for all. This "all" refers to the whole: Earth itself, its inhabitants, and the Universe. It is both the end goal and the road you travel towards it.

In practice, this is the action of living (or trying to live) harmoniously with all of life as it is unfolding. To live in harmony with "the Divine," the natural world, your own self, your loved ones and your community. To me this means seeing beauty and positivity in every person and situation that you come across during each day.

I am still struggling with feeling that same kind of compassionate love for myself.

EVELYN REFINIUS

What is your Instagram handle?
  @evchen_1204

Where are you from originally?
  Düsseldorf, Germany

Where do you live now?
  Village near Frankfurt am Main, Germany

What is your occupation?
  Process Engineer

What are your hobbies?
  Drawing and painting, Yoga, Poetry

When did you first join Songwrite?
  First Songwrite: March 21, 2020

What songs are your lyrics in?
  I don't know for sure if there are any

What's your favorite SP song of all time?
  "Run"

What's your favorite SP song for 2020?
  Not an easy decision, but I think it's "Life On Earth."

What's your Saturday Songwrite story?

  Music and lyrics are the biggest inspiration for my artwork, so it was wonderful to join the Songwrite Sessions and be a small part of the magic of writing a song. I've met lovely, creative, and very talented people because of it and made new friends from all over the world. The Songwrite created a beautiful community of kind, creative, and supportive people. And I love to draw songs: music and the lyrics create pictures in my mind, and I try to draw these.

  I did a drawing for each of the thirteen songs we all wrote together with Gary during the Saturday Songwrite Sessions, and these drawings became a little special drawing series. I collected them in a booklet for my Saturday Songwrite friends to remind us of the lovely time we spent together.

FAYE KELLY

What is your Instagram handle?

@wonderfulfayek

Where are you from originally?

Dublin, Ireland.

Where do you live now?

Dublin, Ireland.

What is your occupation?

I'm a physical therapist.

What are your hobbies?

Music, books, dance.

When did you first join Songwrite?

Week 2

What songs are your lyrics in?

I don't have any of my lyrics in the songs.

What's your favorite SP song of all time?

"Make This Go On Forever"

What's your favorite SP song for 2020?

"Empress"

What's your Saturday Songwrite story?

I started following the lives on the second Saturday. I love the band, and I loved the idea of creating something with Gary and other people. None of my lyrics are in the songs, but it was fun anyway.

Is there anything else that you would like to add about yourself?

I'm not the best writer, but the sessions inspired me to try, at least. It was a great experience, not only for the result, but also for the new friends, and for a good cause.

JACK WILLIAM FINLEY

What is your Instagram handle?

@Jackwilliamfinley

Where are you from originally?

Logansport, Indiana, USA

Where do you live now?

Indianapolis Indiana, USA

What is your occupation?

U.S. Army Retired

What are your hobbies?

Primarily music, writing, reading, photography

When did you first join Songwrite?

...fourth week, I think...maybe.

What songs are your lyrics in?

No lyrics

What's your favorite SP song of all time?

I listened to every album for hours trying to come up with some kind of decent answer for this. I think I narrowed it down to a top...fifteen or twenty, maybe. I think I have a couple more preferences on *Fallen Empires* than I do most of the others.

What's your favorite SP song for 2020?

"Reaching Out To You," or possibly "Empress"

What's your Saturday Songwrite story?

At first I didn't expect the whole Pandemic thing would have a huge effect on my day-to-day life, since I was more or less pretty much an isolationist before all this, but there just seemed to be an overwhelming sense of doom and dread that just seeped into everything as things wore on. I started listening to Alethea's live stuff, and a ton of the older stuff, which always does a pretty reliable job of cheering me up and keeping my spirits high. I used to write quite a bit, but hadn't in several years. Alethea's stuff got me back to thinking more about that, but I didn't really get back to writing much until I followed her to the Saturday Songwrite. I have been writing pretty steadily ever since.

JANA WIEBACH

What is your Instagram handle?

@diejana_80

Where are you from originally?

I was born in Halle/Saale, Germany (back in those days behind the Iron Curtain) and raised nearby.

Where do you live now?

Most boring ... I do still live in Halle/Saale now. But then again: in another country—without moving around!

What is your occupation?

Having studied literature, contemporary history, and media sciences, I'm a cultural scientist by profession. My job, though, is assistant to the Dean of the Engineering Department at a university of applied sciences.

What are your hobbies?

Does being a boys' mom qualify as a hobby?

I'm quite interested in "nerd stuff" like space/astronomy and science fiction, paleontology, ancient times (Ancient Egypt and Greece), lots of cinema and TV series... No gardening (brown thumbs, really), but hanging out outdoors is nice.

When did you first join Songwrite?

I missed two weeks (darn it!) and joined on April 4, 2020.

What songs are your lyrics in? (If any)

In Week 7 or 8 I suggested "dear" (because it does always sound so lovely)—but that doesn't count as a proper suggestion, I guess.

The one line I got into a song is "ocean waves" in Week 9 (Song 10). I realized it when I heard the song for the third or fourth time. Whenever I miss it while re-listening, I panic slightly, thinking I only dreamed this.

What's your favorite SP song of all time?

Leaving aside the obvious options ("Chasing Cars" and "Run"), I'm still torn between "Set The Fire To The Third Bar" and "Shut Your Eyes." I do think that "Set The Fire" is the most intense song ever written...

What's your favorite SP song for 2020?

"Empress." For 2019 and 2020. Being female, I give "Empress" a slight preference to "Life On Earth."

What's your Saturday Songwrite story?

I came across Saturday Songwrite rather randomly on YouTube (while watching tons of SP music and live videos—hardly anything else since the start of the lockdown). I was immediately so impressed and fascinated by the

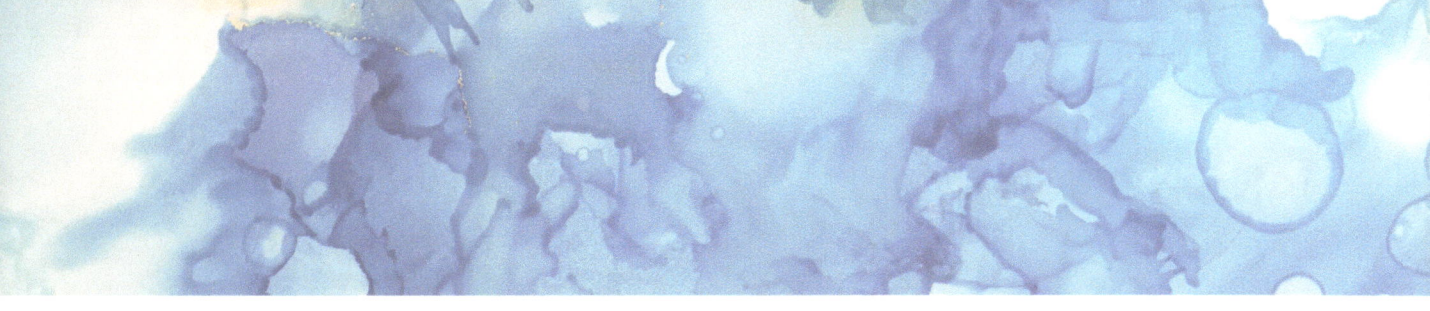

mere idea and the creative process of it (and, well, the generosity of Gary Lightbody doing something like this PLUS all these online live gigs) that Saturday Songwrite (plus the live sessions) were the one and only reason for me to set up an Insta account in the first place.

When joining Saturday Songwrite, I didn't really think of—or hope for—actually getting one of my suggestions into a song. Being part of it was precious enough. It was very unlikely that I would have gotten a line in, because I was absolutely non-strategic: I set aside all logical or planned thinking and suggested words and phrases that would just float into my mind. And every idea I posted only once.

And yet, I finally did get words into a song! Yes! My lucky line is "ocean waves." And while I can't remember most of my lyric suggestions anymore and couldn't have said for most of them why they came to my mind at all, I do know this very well for "ocean waves."

On his Q&A sessions on Thursdays, Gary was quite regularly asked what he was currently reading, watching, or listening to. He always gave lovely recommendations for all of these topics. Among the recommendations for books was *Manhattan Beach*—or, as Gary said in one of the Q&As, "basically anything by Jennifer Egan." Sounded convincing to me! Because good writers tend to recognize good readings when they see them. Gary Lightbody must know, right?

So I got myself *Manhattan Beach* (and then basically every novel written by Jennifer Egan)—it is a great read. So good, I couldn't lay it aside. This book grabs your heart and your mind and makes you think a lot about it. A lot. In this light, "ocean waves" might not be the most brilliant thought, I admit it. There would be better, profounder things to say. But the idea of "ocean waves" spontaneously crossed my mind during this particular week's Saturday Songwrite session, prompted by the reading experience of a book that Gary himself had recommended. Those two little words made their way around half of the world and found their way into a Saturday Songwrite song! They connected the Thursday live gigs to the Saturday Songwrite sessions like a bridge. At least for me, that is what they did.

Is there anything else that you would like to add about yourself?

A Thank You Note for Gary: I will never forget, I will forever be grateful to you for being a lifeline, when everything else that is or was meant to be a lifeline felt like a heavy weight and an inescapable trap. Thank you for being legend and just the way you are.

JANE HOPKINS

What is your Instagram handle?

@Janeymelissa73

Where are you from originally?

I am from a small town called Colwyn Bay in North Wales, UK. I have lived here all my life.

What is your occupation?

I have two grown up sons and I am a primary teacher. I have worked with children and young adults for almost 20 years now, before and after I became a teacher.

What are your hobbies?

I have most recently become interested in reading a lot of different books. I like true life and inspirational books mostly. I have always loved music, and when I was around 30 I started to go to festivals, starting with the best: Glastonbury!! In fact, the very first time I saw Snow Patrol play live was at Glastonbury in 2004. I had been listening to their album Final Straw for a few months and was so excited to see them, as well as being excited to be at the biggest and best festival there is! I fell in love with SP, and then went to see them all over the UK as much as was possible (at least twice a year).

When did you first join Songwrite?

I was very lucky to join Saturday Songwrite at the very beginning, so I never missed a week.

What songs are your lyrics in?

I managed to get a couple of lyrics on two songs:

Week 5 - "On the Edge of All This" - Goodbye darkness (became "Goodbye, dark")

And the other lyric was from a song that isn't on the EP. The lyric was something like a "new chapter." I can't recall exactly which song it was—Week 7?

What's your favorite SP song of all time?

I fell in love when I heard "Run," which I know is an obvious one, but it really struck a chord with me at that time, as I was going through a very difficult period in my life physically and mentally. I would listen to "Final Straw" on a loop and forget all my troubles, just losing myself in the music. Gary's voice is very soothing, don't you think?

What's your favorite SP song for 2020?

I love "Soon." It is a really heartbreaking track, but also full of hope and love. My favourite song from the EP is "Light Years."

JANE HOPKINS (CONTINUED)

What's your Saturday Songwrite story?

I was isolating mostly on my own, because I had a flatmate who spent most of his time with his family. My grown-up sons had both gone away to college and university, so this was the first time in many years I wasn't living with any of my family. The sessions became such a godsend to me. I felt connected to something at such a lonely and difficult time.

Is there anything else that you would like to add about yourself?

I am looking forward to carrying on travelling to different parts of the country—and even other countries—to watch SP. I would love to see them in America. I have travelled to America twice and spent a summer at a camp working in Pennsylvania two years ago. I am planning to go to America again in 2021, and I would love to coincide my trip with a live show.

GARY by Lori Throne

JENNIFER SIMONE

What is your Instagram handle?
>@donkeybiter

Where are you from originally?
>Shenandoah, Pennsylvania, USA

Where do you live now?
>Philadelphia, Pennsylvania, USA

What is your occupation?
>Healthcare

What are your hobbies?
>My dog, traveling, martial arts

When did you first join Songwrite?
>March 2020

What songs are your lyrics in?
>"Light Years"

What's your favorite SP song of all time?
>"Set The Fire To The Third Bar"

What's your favorite SP song for 2020?
>"Get Balsamic Vinegar...Quick You Fool"—it's fitting for 2020! Haha!

Did you submit artwork for the EP cover contest?
>I submitted a photo because I'm much better at photography than drawing.

What's your Saturday Songwrite story?
>I suffer from debilitating anxiety and writing my feelings out was every therapeutic.

Is there anything else that you would like to add about yourself?
>I would just like to add a huge thank you to Gary for creating this opportunity. And the fellow Saturday Songwriters—it was so nice working with you all!

JULIANA SOUZA FLORES

What is your Instagram handle?

@julianaflores.93

Where are you from originally?

I'm from Curitiba, Paraná, Brazil.

Where do you live now?

Campinas, São Paulo, Brazil.

What is your occupation?

I'm an nutritionist.

What are your hobbies?

Reading, music, handicrafts, photography.

When did you first join Songwrite?

I joined in Week 4.

What songs are your lyrics in? (If any)

I don't have any lyrics in the songs.

What's your favorite SP song of all time?

I love "Signal Fire."

What's your favorite SP song for 2020?

"I Think Of Home"

Did you submit artwork for the EP cover contest?

Yes. My friend Camila give me the idea, and I created art for the cover.

What's your Saturday Songwrite story?

My friend Camila posted something about the songwriting sessions, and then I started to participate in the lives. I started to watch in Week 4, but only sent some ideas of lyrics in Week 5. I never had any lyrics in the songs, but just being a part of the process, and being able to interact with Gary, is amazing.

Is there anything else that you would like to add about yourself?

Never been great at writing, but our lives and the moment we are living now helped me to create some art and poetry. Not only that, but the opportunity to chat with Gary, and other people from different places, was amazing.

JULIE BIERLAIRE

What is your Instagram handle?

@JulieBierlaire

Where are you from originally?

Charleroi, Belgium

Where do you live now?

I live in Brussels and in Bastogne (Belgian Luxembourg)

What is your occupation?

I am a social worker—I work to promote children's and young people's rights

What are your hobbies?

Music of course—I play trumpet as well

I am a bookworm! I write a lot as well. I draw, hike a lot, and cook a lot

When did you first join Songwrite?

First Saturday, I love music, I love words, I love collaborative work. It was the perfect project for me!

What songs are your lyrics in? (If any)

"Reaching Out to You"

What's your favorite SP song of all time?

"Don't Give In"—I owe a lot to this song.

What's your favorite SP song for 2020?

"The Curve of Earth." It was a sad, weird, and beautiful Saturday for a lot of us. You can feel it in the song, I think.

What's your Saturday Songwrite story?

I truly believe in collaborative work. In my field, a lot of people like to think they do collaborative work, while they do...the opposite.

With kindness we give the best of ourselves, we feel allowed to be ourselves. We were a team of thousands! But it worked, and we can prove it to the world—it works when we are sincere and when we really want to be collaborative!

To be able to be creative, to live these values with all of you, it means the world to me.

LIZZIE OTTAWAY

What is your Instagram handle?

@stitchanoscar

Where are you from originally?

London, UK

Where do you live now?

Whitstable, Kent, UK via Edinburgh, Scotland

What is your occupation?

Part-time Public Examinations Administrator in a local school for students 11-18 years old.

What are your hobbies?

With my patchwork and quilting I like to work in both mathematical and free-form styles. I love traditional island hand knitting and I also make bobbin lace. I read widely and can play the piano (badly). I take a weekly Pilates class and daily long walks in nature to help control my anxiety. I am owned by an 8-year-old Cockapoo named Oscar and together we are learning how to do dog agility.

When did you first join Songwrite?

Week 1

What songs are your lyrics in?

I couldn't really believe it when across the weeks Gary wrote down a fair number of my lyric ideas. I'm very grateful and honoured that several made their way into some of the songs we wrote together.

One of my "Oh, my goodness" moments was in Week 7 when I suggested, "We are all Mrs. Dalloway." This made Gary smile and laugh out loud as he replied with, "Are we now? I don't know how I would get that in… I'm writing it down anyway." He couldn't, but for those of us lucky enough to have experienced this, there was nothing like hearing him say my words back to me.

There are lyrics of mine in the songs we wrote in:

Week 1 - "Dance With Me" - Alone together

Week 8 - "Reaching Out To You" - Afraid

Week 3 - Hold tight (became "Holding on tight")

Week 4 - "Silver Linings" - All will be well

Week 9 - Some day you will know

Week 10 - Hold on

Week 12 - This is not the end (became "It's not the end of the hunger" and "It's not the end of the fire")

- Still real to me (became "This is still real to me")

- In the dark

Also in Week 7, my lyric suggestion "I find my peace in the woods" triggered nostalgia. As he wrote, Gary spoke this phrase of mine out loud, and then he said it again and again. His response was "There's a… It made me think of Crawfordsburn Country Park. I live beside woods or forest park… I just got homesick there, but anyway." A bit later, someone else contributed "Forest." I like to think that my essence is in the line "Yes, the forest knows what no one else can know." ("The Curve of Earth")

LIZZIE OTTAWAY (CONTINUED)

What's your favorite SP song of all time?

"What If This Is All the Love You Ever Get?"

What's your favorite SP song for 2020?

"Empress"

What's your Saturday Songwrite story?

Serendipity.

All you really need to know about me is that I have always loved (no, adored) R.E.M. I did meet Peter Buck once and, thankfully, didn't embarrass myself in front of him.

In 2010, Peter Buck and Scott McCaughey popped up on the first Tired Pony album which I really liked (just as well because by this time R.E.M. were about to call it a day and I always like to have a Plan B).

Fast-forward through the most trying of years (2013 and 2014), as my long-term relationship broke down and my dear dad died of dementia, to 2015 when I became a singleton. I continue to live alone.

In December 2019, a "blue tick" someone I admire posted a photo from a Royal Albert Hall Snow Patrol gig on his Twitter feed. Rediscovering that I did own a SP album (*Up to Now*), I started following both the band and Gary Lightbody on social media. I have an eclectic taste in music, and Snow Patrol fits in seamlessly.

Following the posting of Gary's online invitation to "Let's write a song together," I revived my dormant IG account and, on Saturday 21 March at 7pm BST, I joined in for the first Saturday Songwrite.

This is what it meant to me: A unique experience that brought calmness, laughter and something to look forward to at a time when nearly everyone was scared and many of us were separated from our family members. Every single one of us shared our experiences of lockdown and our feelings about isolation, love, hope, anxiety, loss, and sadness with complete honesty.

I felt seen and saved by Gary's authenticity, his whimsy, and his love for us all. The live gigs, the Q&As and, above all else, the Saturday Songwrites were beacons of light, refuges and appointments with optimism (and my SSSW friends) in some of my very darkest times.

I know that I owe Gary for my sanity and also for my rekindled creativity. Saying "Thank you" will never ever be enough.

Is there anything else that you would like to add about yourself?

I have synesthesia which, for me, means that I perceive some sounds as colours. Occasionally, this can lead to sensory overload. If I could choose my career again, I would be a falconer (training and flying birds of prey).

It has only been in the last 15 months that I have written anything remotely creative. Being part of Songwrite has helped me enormously to become braver and a wee bit less self-conscious.

I do have one simple wish and that is to meet my Songwrite Sisters in real life (maybe at a Snow Patrol gig). I am just so grateful for you all.

LORI THRONE

What is your Instagram handle?

@A_Lori_Creation

Where are you from originally?

I have lived the majority of life in outer suburbia of the greater Kansas City, USA area

Where do you live now?

Overland Park, Kansas, USA

What is your occupation?

I am a Surgical Technologist working as a lead in Sterile Processing. I have been in this profession for 11 years. Prior to being a Surg Tech, I worked in food service for 20+ years.

What are your hobbies?

My hobbies are painting and drawing.

When did you first join Songwrite?

I was in the Saturday Songwriting sessions from the very beginning, never missing a session.

What songs are your lyrics in?

Although I made numerous suggestions for lyrics, the only thing that made it in were a few chords and the word "Dear," which Gary uses quite regularly throughout his lyrics. But I asked and it happened, so I'll gladly take the credit.

What's your favorite SP song of all time?

My favorite SP song is "Run," because it was my introduction into a brighter, more beautiful world having discovered their music. All in all, I have several favorites depending upon my mood.

What's your favorite SP song for 2020?

It varies, but I think "The Curve of Earth" is in the lead.

What's your Saturday Songwrite story?

I was having a difficult time with what was happening in the world and was starting to slip a bit deeper into my depression, with which I have been struggling for years. I am not very social, don't do too much more than work and create art, but the abrupt halt on living wreaked havoc on my mental state. SP to the rescue! Something fun and wonderful to look forward to each week. Gary was the perfect lifeline, exactly what I needed for my mental health. I have enjoyed being a part of the SSW sessions and have met so many wonderful people along the way.

LOUISE MARIE ROBERTS

What is your Instagram handle?
> @lou.r.botanic

Where are you from originally?
> Phoenix, Arizona, USA

Where do you live now?
> Phoenix, Arizona, USA

What is your occupation?
> Botanist and teacher

What are your hobbies?
> Plants, gardening, books, music

When did you first join Songwrite?
> The first session

What songs are your lyrics in?
> Sadly, I don't have any of my lyrics in songs

What's your favorite SP song of all time?
> "Run"

What's your favorite SP song for 2020?
> "Life On Earth"

What's your Saturday Songwrite story?
> I always loved the band and was already watching the lives that Gary was doing, playing songs. When he started Saturday Songwrite I joined too, and gave some ideas of lyrics that unfortunately he didn't used in any songs. But I've enjoyed the process anyway.

Is there anything else that you would like to add about yourself?
> I'm not the best at writing things that are not related to my job, but I have tried to write poems and lyrics, thanks to Gary's and other fans' inspirational words.

MARGARITA MARTINEZ

What is your Instagram handle?

@gretaeds81

Where are you from originally?

Mexico

Where do you live now?

New Mexico

What is your occupation?

I taught literature and history for ten years. Now I'm an editor.

What are your hobbies?

Reading, writing, concerts, hiking, travel.

When did you first join Songwrite?

From day one

What songs are your lyrics in?

I got a line in Week 12, but I don't know that we ever got a title for the last song.

What's your favorite SP song of all time?

"Daybreak"

What's your favorite SP song for 2020?

"Daybreak." That song is hope and joy distilled down to its purest form.

What's your Saturday Songwrite story?

I caught COVID-19 at the beginning of the pandemic and have been sick with long-term effects ever since. The Saturday Songwriters were an oasis of happiness in a very difficult time. They gave me a community so I didn't feel so alone. That sense of connection continues to endure even after SSW ended. I still have people to walk beside me, even though all my family and friends are far away.

On the Saturday Songwriters Come Dance With Us group on Facebook, I suggested doing #100daysofHeaney, based on an idea I saw on Twitter. People were interested! As of the time of this writing, we're thirty days into the project, reading one poem each day and discussing it. I really enjoy hearing people's different perspectives and seeing some of the poems through an entirely new lens. It's another example of the community formed by SSW, and all the creative potential it has tapped.

As for a more lighthearted SSW story—I'm the person who joyfully declared "Happy Saturday, everybody!" one fine Thursday before a live show, to which Gary gave a very bewildered look and suggested, "You might...want to check your calendar." Pretty much the only time Instagram's algorithm let one of my comments get seen, of course! I fell out of my chair laughing.

Is there anything else that you would like to add about yourself?

Just *thank you*. Thank you to Gary and all the Songwriters. You'll never know the extent to which your compassion kept me going. I hope I can do the same for others.

MARY BETH MAAS

Where are you from originally?

I'm from the same area where I live now—Central Wisconsin, USA—a medium-sized town called Wausau ("the far-away place," from the Native Americans who lived here first). I went away to college in Madison, Wisconsin, but came back because I was getting married and my fiance lived here. I often wish I had moved to a larger place, but I've got friends and family here.

What is your occupation?

I'm a retired special education teacher who taught for thirty-five years at the elementary level. After I retired, I joined AmeriCorps and spent four more years tutoring high-risk high school students, a job I loved.

What are your hobbies?

My favorite things to do are varied: I'm a writer, taking classes at UW-Madison—my favorite genre is historical fiction (nothing published yet but I hope soon!); traveling (visited thirty states and seven foreign countries, England and Ireland the most recent, and I'm going back again when Covid is over); I'm an avid reader, and I like to walk, swim, and lift weights for exercise. Of course music is a huge part of my life. Snow Patrol, Coldplay, and George Michael are special, but I like 60s, 70s, and 80s music—even some 90s like Take That and Backstreet Boys. Eclectic, I guess.

When did you first join Songwrite?

I didn't join Saturday Songwrite until Week 7, and I really regret not joining sooner. I didn't feel I had anything to add; I don't know guitar chords and I didn't understand how it all worked. But once I joined, I loved it. Gary made it so special.

What songs are your lyrics in?

None of my lyrics were used, but I took a few lines of mine to get back into writing poetry, which I did when I was younger. I'm finding that I really enjoy it, so I guess I must thank the Gary and the SSW group for a "new" hobby that I've returned to after many years.

What's your favorite SP song of all time?

How can anyone have one favorite SP song? I guess I would narrow mine down to three, which is still terrifically hard: "You Could Be Happy," "Warmer Climate," and "Open Your Eyes."

What's your favorite SP song for 2020?

"The Curve of Earth," which is an incredibly beautiful ballad and makes me want to cry.

Is there anything else that you would like to add about yourself?

I'm addicted to Snow Patrol for their great music and fun personalities, and I'm half in love with Gary, but aren't we all?

MEL EATHERINGTON

What is your Instagram handle?
>@druidmel / @wanderingbloomart

Where are you from originally?
>Eastern North Carolina, USA

Where do you live now?
>Northern New York, USA

What is your occupation?
>Artist and poet

What are your hobbies?
>Singing, fiber arts, wiresmithing, swimming, reading

When did you first join Songwrite?
>Week 1

What songs are your lyrics in? (If any)
>Week 5 - "On the Edge of All This" - magic mayhem

What's your favorite SP song of all time?
>"Dark Roman Wine" or "Heal Me"

What's your favorite SP song for 2020?
>"Empress"

What's your Saturday Songwrite story?

>The day Snow Patrol announced the cover art winner, I was getting ready to swim with my kids and my mother-in-law. I checked Instagram at 3pm on the dot so I could congratulate the winner before jumping in. Nothing. I waited a minute or two more, but it was a hot and sticky day, so I put my phone down on the deck railing and we all splashed into the water. A few minutes later, one of the kids knocked a toy out of the pool, and I got out to retrieve it. I saw my phone and impulsively decided to look again. I found the post and thought, "Hey, that looks kind of famili--OMG THAT'S MY ART!" Then I started yelling incoherently and dancing around the deck, dripping from the pool, shaking and crying. Everyone in the water thought I'd lost my mind until I finally got the words out that, "They picked me! It's my art on the cover!"

>It's been an incredible journey...life will never be the same. I am profoundly grateful, to put it mildly. As amazing as it's been to have my art on *The Fireside Sessions* album cover, I treasure the friendships made through the Saturday Songwrite process even more.

MERCEDES MCLAUGHLIN

What is your Instagram handle?

@mercedes.mmclaughlin

Where are you from originally?

Philadelphia, Pennsylvania, USA

Where do you live now?

Phoenixville, Pennsylvania, USA

What is your occupation?

Senior Scientist—I edit health technology assessments

What are your hobbies?

Knitting, painting, pottery, writing, walking my dogs, learning to play mountain dulcimer and mandolin

When did you first join Songwrite?

At the start. Gary's inspiring sessions on Instagram with my fellow songwriters awakened my creative spirit from slumber.

What songs are your lyrics in?

In the last song of the last session of SSW (Week 12—yet to be recorded and titled). My lyric "Be my first light in the last dark" changed to "be the light" and also formed the basis of one of my poems.

What's your favorite SP song of all time?

"Lifening" (I tear up every time I hear it—it tugs at my heartstrings)

What's your favorite SP song for 2020?

"Life on Earth" (I love its epic majesty)

What's your Saturday Songwrite story?

I'm a longtime SP fan dating back to the early 2000s. I've always loved Celtic and British folk-rock such as Fairport Convention, the Chieftains, John Martyn, etc., so SP's sound and their lyrics speak to me. Being part of the SSW group has invigorated my creative spirit, and I'm so happy to have made so many new friends around the world.

Is there anything else that you would like to add about yourself?

That's about it!

MIHAELA BERG DIVALD

What is your Instagram handle?
    @bergdivald

Where are you from originally?
    Slavonski Brod, Croatia

Where do you live now?
    Samobor, Croatia

What is your occupation?
    Business administrator

What are your hobbies?
    Astrology, music, rock concerts, reading, painting (abstract fluid acrylic art technique), writing poetry or something like that—lyrics for my soul

When did you first join Songwrite?
    The first SSW, March 2020

What songs are your lyrics in?
    Week 7a - "The Curve of Earth" - gentle touch (in chorus)

What's your favorite SP song of all time?
    "Set the Fire to the Third Bar"
    "Run"
    "Crack the Shutters"

What's your favorite SP song for 2020?
    "Don't Give In"
    "What If This is All the Love You Ever Get"

What's your Saturday Songwrite story?

    I wrote "gentle touch" in "The Curve of Earth" and was really surprised when Gary saw that on screen. He wrote it down in his book, and then said, "Gentle touch... can't spell it, don't have it." After he said that, I thought, *Omg, he doesn't like it!* I was sad about it...but then there it was, in the chorus and I'm so happy about it!

    "The Curve of Earth" is my special song. Every time I hear it, it brings peace and stillness into my heart. I also want to mention my friend Iva Caisa—she made a beautiful lyrics video for song, "The Curve of Earth." (It is on my YouTube channel M Divald; everyone is welcome to watch it and share it with your friends!)

    It represents gratitude from me and my dear friend Iva, and I would dare say from all of us to Gary Lightbody and Snow Patrol and his/their true devotion to make this project happen. It was so hard to get Gary to notice all our suggestions and lyrics. Sometimes I was frustrated because Instagram delayed putting words on the screen. You never knew when Gary would look up and what lyrics he would see. Like Alethea said, not a damn word—we all saw that, and finally Gary too!

    The rest is history.

MIHAELA BERG DIVALD (CONTINUED)

I hope someday someone will make a documentary about Saturday Songwrite and *The Fireside Sessions*, about Gary's genius idea to record songs with his fans.

It is very well deserved.

Fans from all around the world came together in these uncertain times and created something beautiful and for a good cause (Trusell Trust Foundation).

New friendships, new horizons, discovering new parts of me I never knew I had in me.

They say "every crisis is an opportunity in disguise!" For me it really was and still it is true.

Thank you Gary Lightbody!

Thank you Snow Patrol!

Your devoted fan forever, Mihaela!!

Is there anything else that you would like to add about yourself?

> After SSW I started to write my own songs, lyrics, and poetry. It helped me to express my feelings and creativity. I don't think my poetry is something special. I don't expect much from it. I just enjoy doing it, enjoy writing and fluidacryl painting. It's all new to me, but it's a great experience.

MK BRENNAN

What is your Instagram handle?

    mk.brennan

Where are you from originally?

    Western NY, Toronto, Massachusetts - USA

Where do you live now?

    Charlotte, NC, USA

What is your occupation?

    Now retired—I am a Registered Nurse and Massage Therapist

What are your hobbies?

    Writing, painting, making bird baths/plant stands, learning to play my guitar that I bought in February 2020.

When did you first join Songwrite?

    The first Saturday—March 21, 2020

What songs are your lyrics in?

    None, sadly—though I know that he wrote some of my suggestions down. I kept trying to get the word 'ethereal' in, and he did write that down one week. He also wrote one that was basically me just expressing how the Instagram algorithms seemed to be working: "I'm not seeing what you see."

What's your favorite SP song of all time?

    If I can only choose one, it would be "Set Down Your Glass"

What's your favorite SP song for 2020?

    For one *created* in 2020, it would be the one from Saturday Songwrite Week 3. For all that is going on during 2020, I like "Lifening" and "I Think of Home."

What's your Saturday Songwrite story?

    Gratefully, I found out about Gary's plans to do some live sessions through Facebook and Instagram posts. That led to the information about SSW. Early on during SSW, I was able to connect with Courtney and Cindy through comments on one of Gary's posts following a session. Those connections led to creating a "thank you" book for Gary, with Cindy, that contained writings from Songwriters. Since then, the SSW community has grown and now also includes a Facebook group specifically for songwriters where they can share their creative endeavors.

Is there anything else that you would like to add about yourself?

    I am very grateful for the blessings that have come through SSW and to Gary for all of the time, laughter, tears, and caring that he brought to the sessions. The friendships formed around the world have truly opened up and enriched my life. I am looking forward to finally being able to see SP in concert—fingers crossed for 2021!

SHELLEY BLAIR

What is your Instagram handle?

@ladyflame2018

Where are you from originally?

Northern Ireland

Where do you live now?

Northern Ireland

What is your occupation?

Clerical officer

What are your hobbies?

Watching motorbike racing (both trackside and on TV), listening to music, reading, crafts

When did you first join Songwrite?

Week 5 was my first session

What songs are your lyrics in?

Unfortunately, none of my lyrics were picked for the songs, but the first one I ever submitted ("as bright as Venus," which inspired my contribution to this collection) did get a mention from Gary. I couldn't believe it. I didn't even care that it wasn't used in the end, I was just happy that he'd seen it. Talk about beginner's luck!

What's your favorite SP song of all time?

"Just Say Yes," "Run," "How To Be Dead," "Disaster Button," "Open Your Eyes," "Take Back The City"—the list goes on

What's your favorite SP song for 2020?

Either "Reaching Out To You" or "I Think Of Home"—I can't choose!

What's your Saturday Songwrite story?

I joined in during Week 5, and it quickly became one of the highlights of my week, along with the Thursday night gigs. I got ideas from books, magazine, articles etc. and I'd either try to remember them or write them down. It was brilliant to be involved with a project like this and to know that so many other people were joining together every week to try and make something that, now that it's finished and out there, is ultimately going to benefit people.

Is there anything else that you would like to add about yourself?

"I'm a "budgie mum" and I love cake, chocolate, winter (it's my summer!) and Italy! Also: Gary, if you're reading this, I'll never be able to thank you enough for helping to keep me sane and giving me something to look forward to during the lockdown days. Keep being your kind, generous, fabulous self and may the Force be with you always!

SONIA VANCE

What is your Instagram handle?

@Sonia_Vance

Where are you from originally?

Tennessee, USA

Where do you live now?

Maryland, USA

What is your occupation?

Optician

What are your hobbies?

Writing, cooking, photography, travel

When did you first join Songwrite?

Was there from the start

What songs are your lyrics in?

Unfortunately none of mine made it

What's your favorite SP song of all time?

"In The End" and "Don't Give In." Both have saved me

What's your favorite SP song for 2020?

"Don't Give In"

What's your Saturday Songwrite story?

I was saying hello to my friend Paula, and then Gary noticed and said hello to her as well and made her whole day!

Is there anything else that you would like to add about yourself?

Very thankful for this whole experience and for the lovely people involved. In a time where there was so much sadness this was a big bright spot in the lives of so many!

TERRI JOSEPH GARRITY

What is your Instagram handle?
> @terri_joseph_garrity

Where are you from originally?
> Indianapolis, Indiana, USA

Where do you live now?
> Indianapolis, Indiana, USA

What is your occupation?
> Account Manager for a title insurance / escrow company

What are your hobbies?
> Singing, guitar, songwriting/poetry, reading, gardening

When did you first join Songwrite?
> Joined from the very first Saturday and never missed one!

What songs are your lyrics in?
> I have been very blessed to have a lot of my lyrics make it into many of the songs we wrote. Song #11, Song #6, Song #4, Song #3, Song #1 ("Dance w/ Me"), Song #7b, two in Song #8 ("Reaching Out to You"—I also suggested Gary add a bridge, which he did!), and the last song we wrote in Week 12.

What's your favorite SP song of all time?
> "Life On Earth"

What's your favorite SP song for 2020?
> "Heal Me"

What's your Saturday Songwrite story?
> For me, the Saturday Songwrite resparked my creativity, which had been under water for years. I have sung, played, and written since I was 13 and music was always my passion. Nothing brought me greater joy. I was a voice major in college, so it was serious for me.
>
> My beloved husband was seriously ill for the last seventeen years of his life (I lost him in June 2018), and then a week later my father went down (he had been battling Parkinson's/dementia) and I had to put him in a nursing home. I went there daily, all the while working until his passing on Halloween of 2019. I had not the time or energy to do much of anything but work and caregive. So, all that being said, I hadn't really been able to emotionally or spiritually even think about being creative for almost 20 years. I guess I could have, but I didn't. Wasn't my priority. I was/am still dealing with a lot of grief.
>
> And then the pandemic hit, and I was all alone and freaking out (all of my family has passed but I do have wonderful friends). I had to deal with the isolation and the uncertainty and just the general insanity of feeling

my life was just one major devastation after the next. A vast, empty hole with way too much sorrow swirling in and out. Never seeing a light coming, just more darkness.

Then the SSW started that first Saturday, and it was like someone slapped me awake. I was excited. I was engaged. I was stimulated. I found that, yes, I still have it in me to be creative. Not only that, it brought me immense joy and lifted me up and out into the world. Joining this amazing, giving man who brought an entire community of people together during the darkest of times resulted in the incredible music we all made…but it also gifted us love, fun, friendships and ultimately a real sense of family that I believe will endure.

I am beyond grateful and thankful every day to Gary Lightbody. He saved me (his music has always been a comfort and joy) and gave me back a huge part of who I am again. He quite literally helped heal me through all of this. I felt like Gary was my friend, someone who actually cared about me. That feeling grew more and more every SSW, through the gigs and the Q&As. I am in awe of how much love that gentle soul of his emits through everything he says and does. I wonder if he knows just how positive a force of love and light he is to so many people in this world? I hope so.

TIHANA ŠILETIĆ

What is your Instagram handle?

@tihachcro

Where are you from originally?

Zagreb, Croatia

Where do you live now?

Zagreb, Croatia

What is your occupation?

I am a biologist/ecologist and former synchronized swimmer, active still as an international synchronized swimming judge

What are your hobbies?

I am a passionate concertgoer and a music lover. My favourite bands are U2 and Snow Patrol.

When did you first join Songwrite?

I have been a part of Gary's Saturday Songwrite sessions from the first week. I was following all of his online gigs, as well as the "song of the day" appearances. Making comments, sending lyrics, requesting songs to play, asking for covers, and posting questions during impromptu Question and Answers sessions gave me so much joy, laughter, excitement, and happiness—it made lockdown bearable.

What songs are your lyrics in?

Gary never managed to see my lyrics suggestions, but he did read some of my comments regarding melodies, and during the rocket launch.

At the first SSW session, I suggested a few lyrics ideas, but Gary didn't see them. During the second session I participated with more lyrics suggestions, but I still didn't have any luck in Gary seeing them and writing them down. So I decided to use them after that session, and that's how my very first poem came about...in English! It was so much fun, and it made me happy and proud. So this is how my creative journey has started.

What's your favorite SP song of all time?

My favourite Snow Patrol songs are "This Isn't Everything You Are," Dark Roman Wine," "Open Your Eyes," "Perfect Little Secret," and "Crack the Shutters." But there are plenty more...all being equal in my Top 50.

What's your favorite SP song for 2020?

"What If This Is All the Love You Ever Get"

What's your Saturday Songwrite story?

The most funny moment was in Week 4 when, after so many posted comments that he didn't see or read, I wrote, "Hearing 4 again...nah." Of course that was the comment that made through and the one he saw. He commented on "nah" in his witty and

funny way.

In the beginnings of Week 6, Gary said, "Hello Croatia! How it's going?" to my greetings (at least I would like to believe it was my comment), and we also got a wee "Hi Croatia" in Week 7. In Week 8—what became our first single session—my comment that melodies "3 or 4 will be the winners" caught his attention. He laughed and replied, "They can't all be awesome."

In Week 11, Gary saw a few of my comments, but still no lyrics. After reading my comment "We can't all watch the launch," he turned his phone to the rocket launch saying, "If you can't watch it, this is for you," and we collectively watched that historical launch together.

In that session we also had a little "conversation" about which melodies to pick, and I wrote "3, but lift off in 4 is amazing." He read it and played the melody again for a second time, commenting "Yeah, 4 does have a bit of whoosh, like a rocket launch for example." After a minute, he decided, "We'll go with 4! Let's say 4 for now."

Is there anything else that you would like to add about yourself?

Writing poems and playing with words has been an exciting and fulfilling task, a new and interesting world for me. I look forward to writing more beautiful poems and learning new words in the process. I am so excited to be a part of this Patchwork Poetry project!

And one short Thank You for Gary:

Your Saturday Songwrite sessions made me alive and hopeful. They took my mind off of lockdown worries a little and made me feel loved and connected with everyone, as well as keeping me sane and lifting my spirit immensely during this turbulent year. We became one united, creative, supporting family. So thank you…

…for allowing us to be a part of a songwriting process,

…for sharing your joy, happiness, sadness, kindness, respect, and for radiating pure love,

…for showing us your serious, concentrated, confused, or deep-in-thoughts faces,

…for letting your guard down and for opening a window to your soul a little bit more,

…for helping us to find creative sparks in ourselves,

and for making those magical, unforgettable and heartfelt songs with us!

You illuminate everything!

VANESSA POWER

What is your Instagram handle?

@findingmytruth

Where are you from originally?

Comanche, Texas

Where do you live now?

Originally born and raised in a small peanut farming town in Texas, I moved to Albuquerque, New Mexico in 1995 and now call it home.

What is your occupation?

Manager (Vitamin Dept @ Sprouts Farmers Market) and small business owner—Hand to Heart Massage & Bodywork (Licensed Massage Therapist/Natural Therapeutics Specialist)

I have spent most of my life working in various bookstores and health food stores, in order to have the freedom to read, write, travel to see live music, and attend Burning Man each year. I am also a small business owner, as a licensed massage therapist. My life motto is: Stay Curious.

What are your hobbies?

Learning to play the ukulele, reading books/poetry, writing, dabbling in artwork (collage/found object), attending concerts (pre-Covid-19)

When did you first join the Songwrite?

From the very first one! Some Saturdays I had to log on from work on my break to throw in a few lines and then watch the replay once I was home later, but I participated either for an hour, or for the entire session all 12 weeks (Week 11 with the shuttle launch and George Floyd's murder, and the final Songwrite after the release were a doozy!)

What songs are your lyrics in?

I had lines written down on two occasions during the prerelease sessions, but they did not make the final song lyrics. However, several of my suggestions were written down during the final (Week 12) session, and two ideas (chaos and hope) and the line "your heart speaks to mine" made it into the final lyrics!

What's your favorite SP song of all time?

...seriously?!?! This changes daily by my mood. They are my (almost) constant soundtrack with every version of every song and every release compiled into a playlist on shuffle. Currently: "Empress," "The Curve of Earth," "Lifening," "What If This Is All The Love You Ever Get," and "New York."

What's your favorite SP song for 2020?

"Life on Earth"

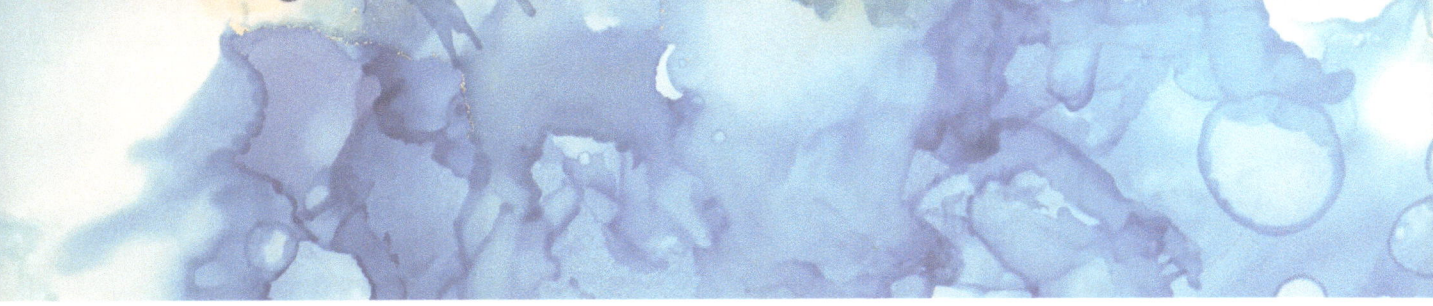

What's your Saturday Songwrite story?

The live Instagram sessions—both the gigs and the Saturday Songwrite—helped me to cope and not feel so alone and isolated in the midst of lockdown, canceled social events, canceled concerts, etc. They inspired me to start writing a lot more poetry, and to actually start typing up, editing, and submitting to publications. I also fell hopelessly further in love and gained another level of respect and appreciation for Gary Lightbody for his amazing creative talent, quick wit, gentle spirit, and world-sized generous heart. The community/family of Snow Patrol fans is the most supportive and positive fanbase of any "celebrity" that I have ever interacted with—just all around good, good peeps! SO REFRESHING!

Is there anything else that you would like to add about yourself?

I was brought back to Snow Patrol with the release of *Wildness*—I heard "Don't Give In" for the first time driving home after having crawled through a window to find that my best friend had died suddenly in his sleep. The entire album, and Gary's recovery story, became the light that I held onto through the most difficult time of my life. No other band will ever mean to me what Gary Lightbody and Snow Patrol do. Life saving. Hope bearing. Joyous celebration. (One of my poems was written during that time—I included it for what SP means to me and the journey they have brought me through.)

I have written poetry as a way to process and capture the events and world around me since I was very young. I have often described my writing style as "snapshot poetry"—my poems are similar to seeing an old photo and remembering the emotions of that moment years later. I had planned to pursue a degree in creative writing, but chose the path of psychology, philosophy, and religious education instead. Most of my writing is in notebooks as unfinished ideas. Only recently have I started committing time to edit, type out, and save my work. This motivation came from the fact that at one point in my life, while in an abusive relationship, my partner destroyed every journal, notebook, and piece of art and writing that I had ever created. I wasn't sure I had it in me to ever start over again.

YARA ARTILES

What is your Instagram handle?

@Yarakaizen94 (for now)

Where are you from originally?

I'm from Spain. I was born in Gran Canaria

Where do you live now?

I live in Spain, but plan on moving to Ireland next year

What is your occupation?

I'm a marketing consultant, but I'll soon be an author as I'll start publishing my own books. Most of them are poetry ones for now, but I'll also write some about marketing and nutrition.

What are your hobbies?

I love writing, listening to music, lifting weights, practicing yoga, learning languages, and new things in general. I love a bit of everything.

When did you first join Songwrite?

Today

What songs are your lyrics in?

I wrote poetry, not songs

What's your favorite SP song of all time?

I have no idea, to be honest. All of them are special. I started learning English when I started listening to them, so I'll always remember both things as something incredibly special.

What's your favorite SP song for 2020?

"Run"

Is there anything else that you would like to add about yourself?

My purpose is making the world a better place by providing the best information I can. I've seen disease and really messed-up things, so raising awareness is key for me.

YOSHIMI MIYAZAKI

What is your Instagram handle?

@yk_miyazaki

Where are you from originally?

Born in Kobe, Japan. As an Army brat, I traveled extensively in my childhood.

Where do you live now?

Corralitos, California, USA

What is your occupation?

In my day job I am an Emotional Intelligence Coach. In my heart I am an author.

What are your hobbies?

Walking on the beach, binge watching TV, cooking, knitting, zooming with friends

When did you first join Songwrite?

Week 1

What songs are your lyrics in?

Sadly, none

What's your favorite SP song of all time?

Yikes! "The Finish Line," "Fallen Empires," "Open Your Eyes," "Reading Heaney to Me," all of "The Lightning Strike," and "You're All I Have"—I am addicted to this one, have to listen every day.

What's your favorite SP song for 2020?

"You're All I Have"

What's your Saturday Songwrite story?

I am new to social media. Both my writing factotum and my social media person tell me that I need to put myself out there more. Yuk. I've done other forms of social media. My third attempt was Instagram, which I found easy to navigate, more intimate, and friendlier. I have made some new friends and thoroughly loved being part of Saturday Songwriters. Remember for a minute Gary was doing a song of the day? That was fabulous. Then it got to be Thursday and Saturday.

As a coach I spend a lot of time up in my aerie on Zoom, with clients. Also writing is a solitary occupation. I spend a lot of time alone so in mid-March, when sheltering in place began in California, the concept was not unfamiliar. I'm an introvert and like my own company. However, as Gary said in April, "We're all looking for quiet, but we don't want it thrust upon us."

I am so grateful to have been part of this process, this joy, laughter, getting to know this fabulous flawed incredibly talented genuine soul who is Gary Lightbody. Thank you to Alethea and MK, who invited us to be part of this book.

YOSHIMI MIYAZAKI (CONTINUED)

Is there anything else that you would like to add about yourself?

> Music is an integral part of my books. I have a section for each book titled simply, "Songs." Each book has a "theme" song and sometimes a specific chapter has a song. There's a magic that happens when a song makes itself known to me—reading a book or watching a TV show or listening to music when I'm writing. I lift my head and know that song is perfect for this book/this chapter. My heart leaps and I am happy. Thank you Snow Patrol—some of your songs are definitely in my books.
>
> I am grateful for the Songwriters putting this together. I appreciate the connections I've made during sheltering in place, and I admire, love, appreciate Gary's time, self-deprecating sense of humor and energy the past few months. The Thursday/Saturday times (as well as the every day times, especially when he did "Reading Heaney" from his front room) helped keep me grounded in this time of uncertainty.

THE SATURDAY SONGWRITERS INVITE YOU TO SUPPORT THESE CHARITIES

Trussell Trust — Supports a nationwide network of food banks and provides emergency food and support to people locked in poverty; campaigns for change to end the need for food banks in the UK.

www.trusselltrust.org

Music for All — They bring 'Learn to Play' experiences free of charge to people of all ages and backgrounds, make grants available to address the musical needs of community music groups and educational organisations, donate instruments and music tuition to individuals who need our help, and promote the life-changing benefits of music making. (Supported by Snow Patrol Hot Sauces)

musicforall.org.uk

Annunciation House — A volunteer organization that offers hospitality to migrants, immigrants, and refugees in the border region of El Paso, Texas.

annunciationhouse.org

Concern America — They work with communities in economically impoverished regions so that community members themselves become empowered to improve their own lives, focusing on health, sanitation, education, and income-generation projects.

concernamerica.org

Concern Worldwide — They deliver life-saving and life-changing interventions to the world's poorest and most vulnerable people. From rapid emergency response to innovative development programming, they go to the hardest to reach places to make sure that no-one is left behind. Founded in Ireland in 1968.

www.concern.net

Furniture Bank — Supports marginalized and displaced families and individuals experiencing furniture poverty. Founded by Sr. Anne Schenck (MK's aunt) in 1998.

www.furniturebank.org

Musicians Foundation — Formed to foster the interests and advance the condition and social welfare of professional musicians and to provide voluntary aid and assistance to professional musicians and their families in case of need. (Est. 1914)

www.musiciansfoundation.org

Sisters of the Lamb of God — An apostolic congregation in France (*Petites Soeurs Disciples de l'Agneau*), America, and Mexico. Canon Law and monastic rules do not provide for the admission of people with mental disabilities to religious life. Through these sisters, this small community is recognized as a public association of lay faithful.

www.facebook.com/sistersofthelambofgod

www.les-petites-soeurs-disciples-de-lagneau.com/en

THE SATURDAY SONGWRITERS INVITE YOU TO SUPPORT THESE CHARITIES

—**ACLU**, www.aclu.org — Their mission is to realize this promise of the United States Constitution for all and expand the reach of its guarantees.

—**Aspire NI**, www.aspireni.org — Works with children in poverty in Northern Ireland, in the hopes of closing the educational attainment gap between the rich and poor. Delighted to support them in providing tuition, sessions and activities for young people.

—**Community Foundation**, communityfoundationni.org — Matching generous people to important causes, manage and award grants to hundreds of charities through donations and funds set up by donors.

—**Cruse Bereavement Care**, www.cruse.org.uk — A leading national charity for bereaved people in England, Wales and Northern Ireland.

—**ENABLE Scotland**, www.enable.org.uk — A Scottish charity working to make life better for people who have a learning disability, and their families.

—**Global Response Management**, www.global-response.org — Exists to bring emergency pre-hospital care and training to those living in or displaced from conflict zones, with a focus on underserved areas.

—**Help Musicians**, www.helpmusicians.org.uk — An independent UK charity for professional musicians of all genres, from starting out through to retirement. They help at times of crisis, but also at times of opportunity, giving people the extra support they need at a crucial stage that could make or break their career.

—**HURT NI**, hurtni.org.uk — Supports people and their families in all stages of recovery from alcohol and drug problems.

—**SAMH**, www.samh.org.uk — Works with adults and young people providing mental health social care support, services in primary care, schools and further education, among others

—**The Trevor Project**, www.thetrevorproject.org — A leading national organization providing crisis intervention and suicide prevention services to lesbian, gay, bisexual, transgender, queer, and questioning (LGBTA) young people under 25.

—**Victim's Voice,** victimsvoice.app — A mobile app that gives victims a legal voice. It empowers people to have happier, healthier lives beyond all forms of abuse.

ALETHEA KONTIS, EDITOR

New York Times bestselling author Alethea Kontis is a princess, storm chaser, and Saturday Songwriter. Author of over 20 books and 40 short stories, Alethea is the recipient of the Jane Yolen Mid-List Author Grant, the Scribe Award, the Garden State Teen Book Award, and two-time winner of the Gelett Burgess Children's Book Award. She has been twice nominated for both the Andre Norton Nebula and the Dragon Award. She was an active contributor to *The Fireside Sessions*, a benefit EP created by Snow Patrol and her fellow Saturday Songwriters during lockdown 2020.

Alethea also narrates stories for multiple award-winning online magazines and contributes regular YA book reviews to NPR. Born in Vermont, she currently resides on the Space Coast of Florida with her teddy bear, Charlie.

Find out more about Princess Alethea and her wonderful world at aletheakontis.com.

MK BRENNAN, EDITOR

MK Brennan has over 40 years of experience in healthcare, including nursing, massage therapy, health promotion, and research methodology. She was the Manager of the Clinical Case Management Department at an acute care hospital and maintained a Massage Therapy private practice for 27 years. She has held roles as the National President for the American Massage Therapy Association and Executive Director of the American Polarity Therapy Association. She currently serves as the Secretary for the Alliance for Massage Therapy Education and is one of the administrators for the Saturday Songwriters Facebook group.

MK is a published researcher and author, editor of textbooks and journal articles, and past Chairperson of the Writing Committee for the Massage Therapy Foundation. She enjoys writing poetry and prose that reflect the experiences of the times—she will be publishing a compendium of poems about topics that came to the forefront during 2020.

MK has three adult sons, two daughters-in-law, two granddaughters, and one grandson due in the coming weeks (as this is written!). Two mixed breed dogs keep her company and active with daily walks.

HEART by Anna Lvova

www.ingramcontent.com/pod-product-compliance
Lightning Source LLC
Chambersburg PA
CBHW050750110526
44592CB00002B/19